THE INFLUENCE OF THE ARTHURIAN ROMANCES ON THE FIVE BOOKS OF RABELAIS

BY

NEMOURS H. CLEMENT

University of California Publications in Modern Philology

Volume 12, No. 3, pp. 147–257

Issued May 8, 1926

University of California Press
Berkeley, California

———

Cambridge University Press
London, England

THE INFLUENCE OF THE ARTHURIAN ROMANCES ON THE FIVE BOOKS OF RABELAIS

By

NEMOURS H. CLEMENT

PHAETON PRESS
New York
1970

Originally Published 1926
Reprinted 1970

Published by PHAETON PRESS, INC.
Library of Congress Catalog Card Number 71-91346
SBN   87753-008-4

THE INFLUENCE OF THE ARTHURIAN ROMANCES ON THE FIVE BOOKS OF RABELAIS

BY

NEMOURS H. CLEMENT

CHAPTER I

INTRODUCTION

Rabelais' literary work, relatively slender though it is, presents such a varied panorama of man and nature that it offers scholarship a fertile field for study and investigation. Rabelais gathered the material that he embodied in his work from all conceivable sources, and he used it with such lavishness and confusion that he has always appeared an enigma to commentators.[1] At first sight his work has the air of a *fatrasie*, a species of composition common in the Middle Ages. In the last two decades, however, scholarship has busied itself more and more with restoring order in this apparent chaos, and several views have been set forth in attempts to show a fundamental and definite plan in the author's mind. Most of these views have been only incidentally expressed in works of a general nature on Rabelais; one has been presented as a formal interpretation of his work. These views are four.

The first is the theory that Rabelais' work is an imitation of the *Macaronics* of Folengo. Louis Thuasne holds to this theory probably more strongly than any other scholar.

---

[1] See Henry Osborn Taylor, *Thought and Expression in the Sixteenth Century* (1920), I, chap. 13: "He has been a much commented on puzzle ever since he lived and wrote that book which seems to hold all life from the cloaca to the heavens."

Tout le roman de Rabelais [he says] se ressent du poème de Folengo, et particulièrement le livre IV. Mais cette influence, plus ou moins sensible, est toujours appréciable. On sent que Rabelais était pénétré de la lecture du *Baldo*, et l'on retrouve dans le *Gargantua* et le *Pantagruel* non seulement des épisodes mais aussi des procédés de composition et d'exposition, et dominant le tout, les mêmes tendances philosophiques et sociales, le même souffle de l'esprit nouveau.[2]

De Sanctis also has expressed the same view in a chapter on Folengo. "Il suo imitatore e continuatore," he says, "è Rabelais che ha la stessa maniera."[3] This view, which is very old, had its origin in the French translation of the *Baldus*, published in 1606. On the title page, under the name of the author, the publisher inserted these words, "Prototype de Rabelais." Lazare Sainéan warmly combats this view:

. . . . des générations de critiques l'ont répété à tour de rôle [he says], et comme les points de contacts réels entre les deux oeuvres sont extrêmement limités, on s'est ingénié à multiplier les rapprochements au risque de tomber dans l'invraisemblance et l'absurde.[4]

But Sainéan, in his zeal to claim for Rabelais a greater measure of originality than he is entitled to, frequently goes beyond bounds and denies the obvious. Charles Lenient makes a more moderate criticism of this theory than Sainéan. He says:

L'auteur du *Gargantua* ne doit guère plus à Pierre Faifeu qu' à Merlin Coccaie. Il leur emprunte comme Molière emprunte à Cyrano de Bergerac. Le talent des écrivains est ici trop inégal pour songer un instant à les comparer.[5]

The second theory is that Rabelais was imitating the *Macaronics*, the popular romances, above all the *Grandes Chroniques*, and the Italian comic romances. This view is sponsored by Jean Plattard,[6] who remarks that the *Macaronics*, appearing in 1517, had gone through three editions by 1532, and the *Morgante* through eleven editions between 1481 and 1531, and that it had been translated into French in 1519. Folengo is mentioned

---

[2] *Etudes sur Rabelais*, 176–177, 202.

[3] *Storia della letteratura italiana*, chap 14.

[4] *Revue des Etudes Rabelaisiennes*, X, 375, at p. 399. See also from the same author, *La Langue de Rabelais*, I, *passim*.

[5] *La Satire en France* . . . . *au seizième siècle* (1877), 59.

[6] *L'Oeuvre de Rabelais*, 1–25.

three times by Rabelais (ii, 1, 7; iii, 2) and the *Morgante*
twice (ii, 1, 30). Plattard categorically affirms the relationship
between Rabelais and the Italian romances in these words:

> C'est de ces épopées heroï-comiques que procède directement la 'Geste
> des Géants' dont Rabelais a fait le cadre de son roman. Ces romans lui
> ont donné l'idée de sa fiction principale, les prouesses des géants. Puis
> d'instinct pour accorder le ton du récit à la nature du sujet traité, il a
> imité quelques traits de la manière de ses modèles.[7]

The third theory is that Rabelais was inspired by the prose
adaptations of the *chansons de geste*, the so-called Romances of
Chivalry. This is the view generally current. It has been held
by Jean Fleury[8] and Heinrich Schneegans,[9] among others, in
the past, and recently Emile Besch[10] and Arthur Tilley[11] have
maintained it in articles on the Romances of Chivalry published
about Rabelais' time. "On peut dire," says Besch, "que le
Gargantua et le *Pantagruel* ne sont d'un bout à l'autre, mais
principalement dans les deux premiers livres, qu'une parodie des
romans de chevalerie." Tilley sets forth this view very succinctly:

> C'est peut-être le commerce avec Nourry qui a détourné Rabelais des
> romans de la Table Ronde, sous l'influence desquels il avait composé ou
> réédité *Les Grandes et inestimables chroniques*, vers les romans fondés sur
> les *chansons de geste* qui ont plutôt inspiré le *Pantagruel*.

Plattard on the other hand thinks that the parody of the Romances of Chivalry is far less developed in Rabelais than in
the Italian romances.

The fourth theory is that Rabelais was inspired by the geo-
graphical discoveries of the day: that in the five books he makes
Pantagruel circumnavigate the globe (*a*) by the route around the
Cape of Good Hope (ii, 24), and (*b*) by the route through the
Northwest Passage. Of the different theories this last has been

---

[7] In *R. E. R.*, X, 375, L. Sainéan refuses to credit Pulci, Bojardo, and
Ariosto with a single borrowing by Rabelais.

[8] *Rabelais et ses oeuvres*, I, 81.

[9] *Geschichte der grotesken Satire*, pt. 2, chap. 1.

[10] *Revue du Seizième Siècle*, III, 155.

[11] *R. S. S.*, VI, 61. See also W. F. Smith, *Rabelais in his Writings*, 20,
21, 27, etc.

elaborated the most.   To it Abel Lefranc devotes an entire book, after having first sketched it in two articles in the *Revue de Paris* (Feb. 1 and 15, 1904).   This theory is the development of a hint Lefranc got from Margry, who, in his book, *Les Navigations francaises et la révolution maritime du XIVe au XVIe siècle* (pp. 225–341), had sought to identify Jamet Brahier, the pilot of the second voyage, with Jacques Cartier, and Xenomanes with Jean-Alfonse de Saintonge.   On the voyage to Utopia in II, 24, Lefranc expresses himself in these terms:

> Il n'est pas douteux qu'en le faisant voguer si loin, Rabelais ait obéi au désir de révéler au prince idéal de la Renaissance la route de l'Inde découverte par les Portugais, et suivie déjà par plusieurs marins de notre pays.[12]

Concerning the voyage to the Dive Bouteille, he says:

> Il [Rabelais] adopte l'itinéraire [the Northwest Passage] passionnément et jalousement cherché par les différentes nations européennes et bravement il le fait réaliser par son héros.[13]

In his book, *Les Navigations de Pantagruel,* he asserts at p. 23:

> D'un côté [the voyage in Book II] et de l'autre [the voyage to the Dive Bouteille] les découvertes géographiques fournissent la trame légère sur laquelle brode la prodigieuse imagination de l'Aristophane moderne, et qu'il ne perd jamais de vue.

These "systems" all explain in varying degrees different aspects of Rabelais' work.   In each case, however, there is so considerable a residue of the five books left unexplained that none of them seems wholly convincing.   More fundamental than any of the theories just sketched, and accounting, it is believed, for a far larger portion of Rabelais' work than any of them, is the thesis herewith set forth:

Rabelais' work constitutes a burlesque imitation of the French medieval romances, but particularly of the romances of the Round Table:

---

[12] *R. de P.,* Feb. 1, 1904.   Cf. Lefranc's views with those of Tilley in the *Mod. Lang. Rev.,* 1906–1910, in a series of articles entitled "Rabelais and Geographical Discovery," now pp. 26–65 in his *Studies in the French Renaissance.*

[13] *R. de P.,* Feb. 1, 15, 1904.

(*a*) Books I and II are an imitation of the Arthurian Romances in general, of which the *Great Prose Lancelot* is a representative specimen;

(*b*) Books III, IV, and V are an imitation of the Grail-quest romances.[14]

---

[14] Not inconsistent with the four theories sketched above and the fifth, proposed by the writer, is the traditional view that Rabelais' work is a *roman à clef.* W. F. Smith, *Rabelais in his Writings*, p. 38, sees the genesis of this idea in the genealogy of Pantagruel (II, 1): ''Rabelais gives fifty-nine giants, making the last two to be Gargantua and Pantagruel, thus for a long time inducing the belief that these two represented Francis I and Henry II throughout, and causing numberless 'keys' to all the characters to be prepared and advocated by their authors.'' Gottlob Regis more than any other has pressed this view in his great edition of Rabelais. Moland, Introduction pp. XLIII–XLIV, gives the key current in the seventeenth century.

CHAPTER II

THE ROMANCES PRINTED UP TO 1553 AND THE REFERENCES TO THEM IN THE FIVE BOOKS

It is too well known to require more than a casual mention that under Charles VIII, Louis XII, and Francis I, an effort was made to revive the spirit of chivalry in France, which indeed seemed for a time to shine with renewed brightness, only quickly to suffer final extinction. The beginning of this effort coincides with the introduction of printing into France; as a consequence, romances were among the chief productions of the new presses. Up to 1553 fully eighty-five of them, not counting translations, were published, and almost all of them went through several editions. *Les quatre fils Aymon* and *Fierabras*, for instance, enjoyed twenty-five editions each in the sixteenth century. Though a few of these romances were of recent composition, like the *Mabrian* and *Le petit Artus de Bretagne*, the greater number were adaptations in prose of old French epics and romances.

These adaptations show two primary types:

First, adaptations of *chansons de geste*. These began to appear about 1430. The adapters made many changes in the old *chansons*, introducing into them elements foreign to them and drawn from the romances of the Round Table. The amorous adventures, the long descriptions of tourneys, and the marvelous, properly the *matière* of the Arthurian Romances, frequently were incorporated and given prominence in these adaptations, which in a few cases were made to fit, and with scant success, into the framework of the Arthurian Romance. The hybrid which resulted is generally known as the Romance of Chivalry. A better name would be Gest Romances, and under this name they are listed below.

Second, adaptations of the romances of the Round Table. In general, these seem to have suffered little alteration at the hands of the adapters, as they already contained the elements which the taste of their readers demanded. The chief change made in them was to rationalize to some slight extent their marvelous, in order to bring it more into harmony with the realistic temper of the times.

Herewith is appended a fairly complete list of the romances of all types which appeared in print up to and through 1553, the year of Rabelais' death.[1] In the column to the right are placed the allusions found in the five books to each one of the romances mentioned in Rabelais.

GEST ROMANCES

Beuves d'Anthone	c. 1500	
Charlemagne et les douze pairs de France	?	
Chronique de Turpin	1476	II, 29: "Ce pendant Panurge contoit les fables de Turpin."
La conqueste de Trebisonde	1483	I, 33: "Allons nous, dist Picrochole, rendre à eux le plus tost, car je veulx estre aussi empereur de Trebisonde."
Doolin de Mayence	1501	
Fierabras (La conqueste du grand roi Charlemagne des Espagnes)		Prologue de l'auteur, Book II: ". . . . 'Fierabras . . . ."
	1486	II, 1: "Qui engendra Fierabras Qui engendra Sortibrant de Conimbres Qui engendra Brushant de Mommiere . . . ."
		II, 30: "Neron estoit vielleux et Fierabras son varlet."

---

[1] Several classified lists of these romances have been attempted, the most complete being that of Ambroise Firmin-Didot, *Essai de classification méthodique et synoptique des romans de chevalerie publiés et inédits* (Paris, 1870). Tilley's list in *R. S. S.* VI, 45, is helpful. See also L. Gautier, *Les Epopées françaises*, ed. 2, II, 609 *seq.*, and Brunet, *Manuel du libraire*, Index. In making this present list the writer has followed chiefly Didot and Tilley. The reader scarcely needs be warned that all the classifications thus far attempted are unsatisfactory.

Galien rethoré	1500	II, 30: "Galien restauré, preneur de taulpes." The *gab* in II, 24, can be only from *Galien rethoré*. But *gabs* frequently occur in the romances: Sommer IV, 266; *Méraugis* ll, 1777 *seq.*
Gérard d'Euphrate	1549	
Girard de Roussillon	1530	
Godefroy de Bouillon: Helyas Enfances Godefroy Antioche Chétifs Jérusalem	 1504	Prologue de l'auteur, Book II: ". . . . Matabrune . . . ." (a character in *Helyas*). II, 30: "Godefroy de Billon, dominotier." "Baudoin estoit manillier." V, 2: "Peu de doubte fismes des enfants Matabrune convertis en cygnes . . . ."
Guerin de Monglave	1518	II, 1: "Qui engendra Roboastre . . . ." (a character in *Guerin de Monglave*).
Huon de Bordeaux	1513	Prologue de l'auteur Book II: ". . . . Huon de Bordeaux . . . ." II, 1: "Qui engendra Galaffre . . . ." (a character in *Huon de Bordeaux*). II, 30: "Huon de Bordeaux estoit relieur de tonneaulx."
Jourdain de Blaives	1520	
Mabrian, fils de Renaud	1530	
Maugis d'Aigremont	c. 1537	
Meurvin, fils d'Ogier	1539	
Milles et Amis	c. 1503	
Morgant le géant	1519	II, 1: "Qui engendra Morgan . . . ." II, 30: "Morgant, brasseur de bière." II, 30: "Il le declaira heretique et l'eust fait brusler vif n'eust esté Morgant . . . ."
Ogier le Danois	1498	II, 1: "Qui engendra Bruyer, lequel fut vaincu par Ogier le Danois . . . ." II, 23: "Peu de temps aprés, Pantagruel ouit nouvelles que son pere Gargantua avoit esté translaté au pays des Phées par Morgue, comme fut jadis Ogier et Artus . . . ." II, 30: "Ogier le Danois estoit fourbisseur de harnois."

Les quatre fils Aymon:
Part 1, Renaud de
    Montauban
Part 2, Maugis d'Ai-
    gremont   1480

I, 27: "Jamais Maugis hermite ne se
porta si vaillammant a tout son
bourdon contre les Sarrasins, des-
quelz est escriptz es gestes des
quatre filz Aymon . . . ."

II, 30: "Les quatre filz Aymon,
arracheurs de dents."

Prologue de l'auteur, Book III: ". . . .
je feray . . . . ce que fit Regnauld de
Montauban . . . ."

ROMANCES OF ANTIQUITY

Apollin, roi de Tyr	?	
La destruction de Jerusalem	1491	
Eneide	1481	II, 30: "Dido vendoit des mousserons."
Florimont	1528	
Hector de Troye (an episode from *Recueil des histoires de Troye*)	?	
Hercules (an extract from the *Recueil de Troye*)	1502	
L'hystoire d'Alexandre	1506	
Jason et Médée	1474	
Judas Machabée	1513	
Les neuf preux	1487	
Les sept sages	1492	
Les trois grands	?	
Recueil des histoires de Troye	1529	
Virgile	?	

ARTHURIAN ROMANCES

Clériadus et Méliadice   1495

Giglan, fils de Gauvain, et
  Geoffroy de Mayence   1530   II, 30: "Giglan et Gauvain estoient
                                  pauvres porchiers."

Gyron le courtois (second
  part of *Palamèdes*)   1501

L'hystoire du Saint Graal,   To *L'hystoire*, to the *Lancelot*, and
  ensemble La Queste dudit   possibly to the *Perceval* must be
  Saint Graal. The *Hystoire*   referred the passages relative to the
  is derived from three   Holy Grail in IV, 42, 43, and V, 10.
  sources:
    1. Le Grand Saint Graal
    2. Perlesvaus
    3. La Queste du Saint
       Graal[2]   1516

Lancelot du Lac: I, 14: ". . . . Gualehaut . . . ."
  Parts 1 and 2, the Lance-   II, 1: "Qui engendra Gallehault . . . ."
    lot proper—the *enfances*   II, 23, See under *Ogier le Danois* above.
    and *Guenevere*   II, 30: "Lancelot du Lac escorcheur
  Part 3, Agravain the   de chevaux morts."
    Proud
  Part 4, La Queste du
    Saint Graal
  Part 5, Morte Arthur   1498
Merlin avec les Propheties   1498 I, 58: ". . . . le style est de Merlin le
                                     prophete . . . ."

Méliadus de Leonnoys (first
  part of *Palamèdes*)   1532
Le noble chevalier Gauvain   1540
Perceforest   1528   II, 30: "Perceforest porteur de
                        coustrets . . . ."
                       II, 30: "Il rencontra Perceforest
                        pissant contre une muraille."

Perceval le Gallois (pre-
  ceded by l'Elucidation du
  Saint Graal)   1530
Le petit Artus de Bretagne   1493   II, 30: "Artus de Bretaigne estoit
                                       gresseur de bonnetz."

Pontus et Sidoine   ?
Tristan, fils de Méliadus   1489
Ysaie le Triste   1522

---

[2] The *Grand Saint Graal* is the work Sommer calls the *Estoire du Saint Graal*; this *Queste* is not the *Queste* forming Part 4 of the *Lancelot*, it is an abridgement of the *Perlesvaus* and the *Queste* of the *Lancelot*.

ROMANCES OF ADVENTURE[3]

Baudoyn, comte de Flandre	1478	
Berinus	1521	
La Chastelaine du Vergier (de Vergy)	1540	
Clamades et Claremonde	1480	
La Conqueste de Grèce par Philippe de Madien	1527	
La Conqueste que le Chevalier Coeur d'Amour fist d'une dame appelée Doucemercy	1503	
Eurial et Lucresse	?	II, 30: "Lucresse, hospitaliere."
Florent et Lyon	1532	
Geoffroy à la grant dent	1525	II, 5: "En aprés lisant les chroniques de ses ancestres, trouva que Geoffroy de Lusignan, dict Geoffroy à la grant dent . . . ."
Gerard de Nevers (Roman de la Violette)	1520	
Guerin mesquin	1530	
Guillaume de Palerme	1552	
Guy de Warwich	1525	
Helayne de Constantinople	1528	
Jehan de Paris	c. 1525	II, 30: "Jehan de Paris estoit gresseur de bottes."
Jehan de Saintré	1517	
Le livre des trois fils de roi	1501	
Melusine	1478	II, 30: "Melusine estoit souillarde de cuisine." IV, 38: "Là trouverez tesmoings vieulx . . . . lesquelz jureront . . . . que Melusine, leur fondatrice, avoit corps feminin jusques aux boursavitz, et que le reste en bas estoit andouille serpentine ou bien serpent andouillicque."
Paris et Vienne	1487	
Philandre	1544	

[3]Here taken in two senses, (a) ''aventure d'amour'' and (b) chivalric adventure unconnected with knight-errantry. These two elements are often found mingled, as in *Mélusine* and *Jehan de Saintré*.

Pierre de Provence	c. 1478	
La plaisante histoire du Chevalier doré et de la pucelle surnommée Coeur d'acier	1542	
Richart, fils de Robert le Diable	c. 1530	
Richard sans peur	1540	
Robert le Diable	1496	Prologue de l'auteur, Book II: ". . . . Robert le Diable . . . ."
Syperis de Vinevaulx	1540	
Theseus de Cologne	1534	
Valentin et Orson	1489	II, 24: "Et ne crains ni traict, ni flesche, ny cheval tant soit legier, et fust ce Pegase ou Pacolet . . . ." (Pacolet is an enchanter who rides a magical wooden horse in *Valentin et Orson*, chap. 24.)

UNCLASSIFIED[4]

Bayart	?
Bertrand du Guesclin	c. 1480
Le Chevalier délibéré	1493
Chronique de Normandie	1487
Maistre Renart et Dame Hersent	?
Passages de outremer de Godefroy	1505
Le Roman de la Rose	1485
La Toison d'or	1516

In addition to the foregoing French romances, the following romances were translated from the Spanish between the years 1530 and 1553:

Amadis de Gaule (first four books)	1540–1544	⎫
Amadis de Grèce	1546	⎪
A sequel to Amadis de Grèce	1548	⎬ by Herberay des Essarts
Esplandian	1544	⎪
Flores de Grèce	1552	⎪
Perion et Lisuart de Grèce	1548	⎭

---

[4] Didot calls these (with the exception of *Bayart*, which he does not list) "Chroniques fabuleuses ou romanesques."

La déplorable fin de		
Flamète	1535	by Maurice Scève
Florisel de Niquée	1552	by Gilles Boileau
Suite de Florisel	1552	by Jacques Gohory
Primaléon de Grèce	1550	by François de Vernassal
Le jugement d'amour	1530	
Méliadus, le Chevalier de la Croix	1534	
Olivier de Castille	1482	
Palmerin d'Angleterre	1553	
Palmerin d'Olive	1546	by Jean Maugin

Tabulating the conclusions deducible from the preceding list, we find that Rabelais was acquainted with as many as twenty-five romances which, from the allusions he makes to them, are to be distributed as follows:

The romances he read with certainty	The romances he read with reasonable certainty	The romances he probably read	The romances that possibly he read

GEST ROMANCES

Fierabras	Chronique de Turpin	La Conqueste de Trebisonde
Galien rethoré		
Godefroy de Bouillon		
Guerin de Monglave		
Huon de Bordeaux		
Morgant le géant		
Ogier le Danois		
Les quatre fils Aymon		

ROMANCES OF ANTIQUITY

Enéide

ARTHURIAN ROMANCES[5]

Lancelot du Lac	Artus de Bretagne	Giglan, fils de Gauvain	Gauvain
Merlin	L'hystoire du Saint Graal		
Perceforest	Perceval		

ROMANCES OF ADVENTURE

Geoffroy à la grant dent	Jehan de Paris	Robert le Diable	Eurial et Lucresse
Melusine			
Valentin et Orson			

The preceding list and table show how extensive was Rabelais' acquaintance with the romances so greatly in vogue in his time, yet neither indicates his real indebtedness to them. Of the twenty-five romances in the table, nineteen are mentioned in the *Pantagruel.* It is clear, consequently, that when Rabelais wrote the second book he was greatly preoccupied with the romances. The purpose of this study is to show that they influenced very profoundly not only the *Pantagruel* and the *Gargantua,* but the remaining three books as well, and to allocate to each of the various types of romances its due proportion of influence in Rabelais' work.

---

[5] The not inconsiderable knowledge of the Grail that Rabelais exhibits would seem to indicate that he must have used other romances as sources besides the *Lancelot* and the *Merlin.* In neither of these, for instance, is the Grail endowed with prophetic power, whereas it possesses this power in *L'hystoire du Saint Graal.*

Nor need it be concluded that Rabelais read only printed romances, as evidence is not wanting that the romances were read in manuscript for some time after they appeared in print. For example, in the early part of the sixteenth century was composed a *Coutumes des chevaliers de la Table Ronde,* in the foreword of which the author tells us that he collected the names and the arms of the knights of the Round Table "tant au livre que Maistre Helye, maistre Robert de Boron, maistre Gautier Moab, ou Le Bret, et maistre Rusticien de Pise en parlent en leurs livres de ceste matière là ou sont escriptz les grands faits de tous les chevaliers de la Table Ronde.'' The Le Bret the author mentions is undoubtedly *Li Contes del Brait Merlin,* often called ''le livres dou *Bret,*'' ''le *Bret,*'' or ''le livre du *Bret,*'' which was never printed and has completely disappeared, even in manuscript form.

CHAPTER III

EVOLUTION OF THE FIVE BOOKS

I

BOOKS I AND II

It is obvious even from a cursory reading of Rabelais that his work falls into two distinct parts—Books I–II, and Books IV–V—which are very loosely joined together by a transitional book —Book III. The chief *matière* of the books of the first part is the *matière* of such Arthurian Romances as the *Lancelot* and, in a minor measure, of the Gest Romances: the *enfances* of the hero and his exploits in war and in peace hold the chief place in them. We are justified in saying that almost all the *matière* of the second part is the *matière* of the Grail-quest romances, parodied, of course, and apparently different from the usual quests, nevertheless showing distinctly its filiation and ancestry.

The question that immediately suggests itself is: Why this lack of coherence and unity? The answer is that Rabelais, when he composed the first part of his work, and not only the first part but each of its two books, had no idea at all of going beyond that part, or each of the books constituting it.

It is now universally admitted that the first piece of writing to which Rabelais addressed himself was the composition, possibly, or, at all events, the retouching, of one of the numerous

---

It is thought that *El Baladro del Sabio Merlin,* printed at Burgos in 1498, contains passages from *Li Contes del Brait.* On this see James Douglas Bruce, *The Evolution of Arthurian Romance* (Göttingen and Baltimore, 1923), I, part iii, chap. 8, and notes.

Naturally the reader need not be warned that the table (pp. 159–160) purports in no manner to be final. In many cases Rabelais' allusions to the romances are too fragmentary to form a basis for anything more than conjecture; and besides it is possible, and even probable, that he read romances that have left no traces in his work.

popular romances of the day, the *Grandes Chroniques*. If we may accept his word for it, this venture was unusually successful: "....il en a esté plus vendu par les imprimeurs en deux mois qu'il ne sera acheté de Bibles en neuf ans," he tells us in the prologue of the *Pantagruel*. It is a fair inference that the success of this *coup d'essai* suggested to, and emboldened, him to continue the story of the gest of Gargantua. This genesis of the *Pantagruel*, the first of the five books, from the chap-book literature of the time is amply attested on page after page. Accordingly, in this, the first book wholly of Rabelais' own invention, two different influences manifest themselves, the popular and burlesque, and the literary.

Among the popular and burlesque elements might be cited Rabelais' lack of measure,— that is, his lack of literary balance as well as of balance in invention — his minute descriptions, and the means which he employs in order to impart to his story an authentic air: the introduction into his narrative of real personages, places, and local natural curiosities. As examples of want of literary balance might be adduced Pantagruel's very extraordinary size (ii, 32), a size beyond that of any giant of story or legend before or since; the interminable coq-à-l'âne in the suit between Baisecul and Humevesne (ii, 11–13), and the debate between Panurge and Thaumaste (ii, 18–19) ; as specimens of want of balance in invention, Panurge's prank on the Parisian lady (ii, 22), his wall about Paris (ii, 15), and the story of how Pantagruel engendered the pigmies (ii, 27). In *Pantagruel* 14 we find several examples of minute description: the number of cows required to furnish Pantagruel with milk, and the size of the saucepan used in cooking his gruel. Illustrations of authentications are the crossbow of the youthful Pantagruel, which today is called the "crossbow of Chantelle"; the huge rock which he placed in a field near Poitiers and which "presently is called the Raised Stone" (ii, 5) ; and the bronze spheres in which the doctors descended into Pantagruel's stomach, "one of which is in Orleans on the belfry of the Church of the Holy Cross" (ii, 33). True, this way of authenticating a story or one of its

incidents is frequently met with in the literary romances, but
the authentications of the *Pantagruel* are obviously of popular
provenance.

Chief among the literary influences are the prose adaptations
of the Old French epics and the Arthurian Romances, Folengo's
Macaronics, and Lucian's *True History* and his *Necyomantia.*
The influence of the Arthurian Romances is apparent in the
framework of the *Pantagruel*: in the ancestry, birth, youth,
appareling, education, and exploits of the hero; the influence of
the *Macaronics* is manifest in several of the characters of Rabelais: Panurge in a great many respects closely resembles Cingar,
Carpalim is none other than Falchettus, Eusthenes is Fracassus,
and Pantagruel's central position with relation to his companions
is very much like that of Baldus;[1] the influence of Lucian is
obvious in the descent of Epistemon to Hell (ii, 30), in the
exploration of Pantagruel's interior by Maître Alcofribas (ii,
32–33), and in the promise of a continuation of the adventures
of Pantagruel and his companions.[2]

In the last chapter of the *Pantagruel* Rabelais promises his
readers a sequel: "vous aurez le reste de l'histoire à ces foires de
Francfort prochainement venantes...." The promised continuation apparently was to be a parody of incidents from the
Orlando furioso,[3] from the *Macaronics,*[4] from Lucian's *True History,* and of the marvelous accounts of the explorers of his day.
Some scholars have looked upon this promise as a mere flourish,
others have taken it seriously.[5]

Two considerations would lead us to regard this promise as
a whimsicality of Rabelais'. The first is the statement that the
sequel would be offered for sale at the Francfort Fair. The

---

[1] W. F. Smith, *Rabelais in his Writings,* 29; Thuasne, *Etudes sur Rabelais,* 159–265.

[2] Lucian, *The Necyomantia; The True History.*

[3] "Comment il espousa la fille du roy d'Inde dict Preste Jean," cf. *Orl. fur.* XXXIII, 96 *seq.,* "et comment il visita les regions de la lune," XXXIV, 67 *seq.*

[4] "Comment il combattit contre les diables....et rompit quatre dents à Lucifer," *Macaronics* XXIII–XXV.

[5] Lefranc, *Les Navigations de Pantagruel,* 25–26.

Francfort and the Lyons fairs determined during the sixteenth century the time of the publication of books for Germany and France respectively.[6] The *Pantagruel* was offered for sale at the Lyons Fair[7] in the fall of 1532. Before this sequel was offered to the public, before it was known what reception it would be accorded, and in view of that accorded to the *Grandes Chroniques,* why should Rabelais have contemplated launching his promised continuation elsewhere, and above all in a foreign country? The question implies its own answer: it was the last of a long series of drolleries. Germany, besides, was not the place to hold out any promise of success to books in a foreign language. Some publishing centers of Germany, notably Strassburg, could vie with Paris or Lyons or Venice or Rome in the number of books they printed. But with very few and very unimportant exceptions the books issued from the German presses were German or Latin.[8] Up to 1625 only eight French books were published at Strassburg, and these, it is believed, emanated from a small French colony in that city.[9] The little town of Frankenthal, in Bavaria, published more French books than Nuremburg, Heidelberg, Oppenheim, and other neighboring cities put together, and up to 1625 the French publications of Frankenthal numbered only ten. It is not at all necessary to concede to Rabelais any extensive bibliographical knowledge to conclude that he could never really have entertained the chimerical idea of launching outside of France any continuation he had in view. Accordingly, he must have been purposely writing nonsense with respect to the sequel he promised.

---

[6] Lefranc, *R. E. R.,* IX, 151; James W. Thompson, *The Frankfort Book Fair,* chap. 2.

[7] George Haven Putnam, *Books and their Makers During the Middle Ages,* II, 9 *seq.:* ''They [the publishers of Lyons] gave attention to the production of books of light literature, such as popular romances, legends, folk-songs .... at a time when the printers of Paris .... and of nearly all the other book-manufacturing cities of Europe were devoting their presses exclusively to theology and the classics. Other cities that interested themselves in light literature were Bruges and London.''

[8] Thompson, p. 31. At p. 79 Thompson says: ''Probably the first Parisian book dealer to come to Frankfort was Jacob de Puys, who came some time after 1540.''

[9] Le Bibliophile Jacob, *Recherches bibliographiques,* 81.

The second consideration is that in books with a grotesque
or marvelous theme the promise of a continuation is almost *de
rigueur*. Rabelais had two such promises under his eyes when he
wrote the *Pantagruel*. In the concluding sentence of his *True
History* Lucian says: ''What next ensued upon the firm land I
shall give a circumstantial account of in the following books.''
Tooke, in a note to his translation, sagaciously remarks: ''It is
highly proper that a history made up entirely of lies should conclude with a promise which the author never intends to keep.''
The other promise is Folengo's. Twice in the course of the
Baldus Folengo promises a harrowing of Hell by Baldus and his
band (X, 545–547; XXI, 207–208). Not having kept his promise,
by the end of his romance, he closes his book with this valedic-
tory:

> Balde, vale, studio alterius te denique lasso,
> cui mea forte dabit tantum Pedrala favorem,
> ut te, Luciferi ruinantem regna tyranni,
> dicat, et ad mundum san salvum denique tornet.

XXV, 651–654.

It is probably this continuation that Rabelais had in mind when
he records among the books of the library of Saint Victor one by
Merlinus Coccaius, *de Patria diabolorum* (II, 7; III, 11).

The *Pantagruel* was very successful, since in the year 1534 it
was going through a fifth edition. Success encouraged its author
to ply once more his pen, and in 1534 the *Gargantua* appeared.
Of the five books it is the best: it has fewer tiresome passages;
its interest is better sustained; it excels the others in construction
and style; it is the most philosophical; in imagination and technique it shows a remarkable superiority over its predecessor; it
avoids the exaggerations that disfigure the *Pantagruel*. In fine,
the *Gargantua* is far less popular than the *Pantagruel,* and much
more closely approximates the literary romances.

Not only in manner and form does the *Gargantua* differ from
the *Pantagruel,* thus exhibiting its independence in conception,
but in two details which are noteworthy enough. The first is

that in II, 23 we are told Gargantua is king of Utopia, which is
generally placed in Asia but may be in Africa (II, 2), whereas in
the first book he is lord of one of the numerous small kingdoms
of France (I, 1). The other is that in the second book (chap. 23)
we learn that Gargantua is dead, whereas in the four other books
he is resurrected without a word and takes a primary part (Book
I), or a secondary part (Books III, IV, V) in the story.

All these considerations prove that the *Gargantua* cannot
possibly be regarded as a continuation of the *Pantagruel* in any
true sense of the term. It is an absolutely independent work
suggested by the success of the *Pantagruel*, just as the latter
itself was suggested by the success of the *Grandes Chroniques*.
And even as the *Pantagruel* did not really look beyond itself
toward a sequel, so again the *Gargantua* was regarded by its
author as his final contribution to the cycle Plattard calls "la
geste des Géants." Rabelais' abstention from writing for eleven
years after the equally successful *Gargantua* would seem to lend
color to this view. In further support of it may be adduced
his acquiescence in the *Disciple de Pantagruel*, which first appeared in 1538 as a companion to pirated editions of the first
two books, and purported to be the promised continuation of the
second book. Some scholars reject its attribution to Rabelais,
others defend it.[10] Among these is Lefranc,[11] who supposes it
was a popular romance of Rabelais', in the manner of the
Grandes Chroniques, designed as a provisional continuation to
Book II. Tilley succinctly states the two views:

Its correspondence with the sequel which Rabelais had promised to the
Pantagruel, and the fact that some of its episodes were borrowed by Rabelais for the acknowledged continuation of his story [Bringuenarilles, L'Isle
Farouche, L'Isle des Ferremens] suggest that he himself was the author.
On the other hand, its wholly popular character, its lack of any of the
higher qualities which distinguish the master's recognized work, and certain
marked differences in style have led the majority of critics to reject the
theory of Rabelais' authorship.[12]

[10] See Josef Schober, *Rabelais' Verhältnis zum Disciple de Pantagruel*
(Wurzburg dissertation, 1904).

[11] *Les Navigations de Pantagruel*, 31, 144, 193 and note.

[12] *Fançois Rabelais*, 220.

If the *Disciple* is not the work of Rabelais, whose is it then, and what explains Rabelais' complaisance in regard to it? At the end of the 1546 edition of the *Disciple* there is a burlesque *privilège* in which appears a long list of proper names applied to familiar animals and objects, each followed by its common name, the last term of the enumeration being *Quentin l'oeuf*. This would seem to indicate a signature: Quentin is the source (the egg, from the Latin *ab ovo, ex ovo*) whence proceeds all that has preceded. This Quentin would most probably be Jean Quentin, who is mentioned in III, 34, as having taken a part in "la morale comédie de celui qui avoit espousé une femme mute." There is reason to believe that on a later occasion still Quentin turned his attention to Rabelais' work. Louis Cons, in the *Revue bleue* of April 25, 1914—before the confirmatory evidence contained in the *privilège* to the *Disciple* came to his attention— hazards the conjecture that he might be the person who retouched the fifth book. He bases his conjecture on these considerations:

The first edition of Book V appeared in 1562 under the title of *L'Isle Sonnante;* the second and complete edition appeared in 1564 with thirty-two additional chapters. A close examination of the passages of Book V, in which appears *la Quinte* or *Quinte,* leads to the conclusion that the word is not an abbreviation of *quintessence* but a disguised signature.

(*a*) The first time that the word occurs with appearances of being a signature is in the heading of chapter 18: *Comment nostre nauf fut encuarquée et fusmes aidés d'aulcuns voyageurs qui tenaient de la Quinte.* In the same chapter these same travelers are again adverted to as "tenant de la Quinte."

It has frequently been noted that from chapter 18 on there is a palpable change in the style of Book V: the narrative limps along, the diction changes, and the direct discourse becomes obtrusive. It is to be borne in mind that this sudden change in style follows close upon the part of the book published in 1562 as *L'Isle Sonnante.*

(*b*) If *la Quinte* or *Quinte* is a signature, there should be some likelihood of finding it in an appropriate place—at the end of the book. Now, at the end of the 1564 edition there appeared an epigram with the conclusion, or rather signature, NATURE QUITE.

The first letter of *Nature* plus the word *Quite* again gives *Quinte,* and the letters *-ature* are a simple anagram of the word *auteur.* Accordingly Nature Quite = Auteur Quinte.

(*c*) At the end of chapter 37 of the 1564 edition there occurs this Greek sentence, followed by its translation:

PROS TELOS AUTON PANTA KINEITAI

Toutes choses se *mouvoient:* a leur fin.

In the French rendering, two striking peculiarities present themselves, (1) the Greek *Kineitai,* an indicative present, is translated by an imperfect, (2) this imperfect is followed by a colon.

In this double peculiarity Cons sees a humanist's ruse to fix attention on the word *Kineitai,* which is once again the word *Kinte, Quinte,* plus the letters I and A, suggesting the name Jean. In this Greek sentence Cons sees the equation,

Pros telos auton panta kineitai = Tout ce qui est d'ici à la fin est l'oeuvre de Quinte.

From these considerations Cons makes three deductions:

First, in chapter 18 the anagram *Quinte* and its context mark the place where began the activity of a *collaborator.*

Second, chapter 38 marks off a second region where appears the intervention of a *continuator.*

Third, the collaborator and the continuator are one and the same person, Jean Quentin.

Cons buttresses his identification with the following arguments:

(*a*) The Cotirail mentioned in chapter 18 is Cotereau, a canon of Notre Dame, and Quentin's most intimate friend.

(*b*) In chapter 20 the author speaks of himself as having "dans le silence en Egypte mordu ses ongles et sa tête grattée," and as having offered in silence sacrifices with the "pontifes de Hieropolis." In these words Cons sees an allusion to Quentin's travels in Egypt and Turkey.

(*c*) Jean Quentin had the erudition and the wide reading necessary to intervene in Rabelais' work.

Cons' final conclusion is: The fifth book, published in 1562 and 1564, is the twice posthumous work of Rabelais and of Jean Quentin, who died in 1560.[13]

Quentin and Rabelais were old friends. In Quentin's youth we find him at Fontenay-le-Comte, where he frequents with Rabelais the circle of the Abbé Ardillon. He traveled in the Orient and became a *chevalier servant* of the order of Malta at Jerusalem. Returning to France he took orders and in 1536 was made professor of Canon Law at the University of Paris. His works comprise books of travel, on navigation, and commentaries on the canonists.[14] If indeed he is the author of the *Disciple* we can readily account for Rabelais' tolerance of, or rather partiality for, it: it was a 'continuation' made by an old friend, which he himself had never had the idea of writing, and which in no wise could be prejudicial to him; further, Quentin at the Sorbonne was a friend in the camp of the enemy, whose influence and protection some day might stand him in good stead. We know that Rabelais did not show the same amiability towards another friend, Dolet, with respect to his unauthorized edition in 1542 of the first two books.

---

[13] See Plattard in *R. S. S.* II, 279. Cons has since accepted in large measure the objections raised by Plattard against his conjecture. Plattard nevertheless recognizes the interest offered by a study of the friendship of Rabelais and Quentin, and of the possible collaboration of the latter in Book v.

[14] *Rev. bleue*, April 25, 1914.

II

BOOKS III, IV, AND V

The first indication to be found of a plan in Rabelais is in the third book. Only the third book looks beyond itself and to the following books. Unlike Books I and II, it is not a unity in itself, but by its form necessarily implies a continuation. There is every reason to believe that before he put his hand to Book III Rabelais had carefully thought out Books IV and V.

In the first place, the journey to the Dive Bouteille is announced in III, 47; and in IV, 1, we learn "[Ils] firent le voyage de Indie superieure en moins de quatre mois,"a time limit to which the author scrupulously adheres. It is not easy to follow the chronology of Pantagruel's itinerary. At times Rabelais is at pains to give the precise duration of a lap of it (IV, 2: ".... au quatrième [jour] découvrirent une isle";IV, 5: ".... au cinquième jour jà commençans tournoyer le pole," etc., etc.) ; at times he indicates the passing of time in general terms (V, 11: "Quelques jours aprés passasmes condemnation,") ; frequently the lapse of time is not indicated at all—for instance, we can gather no idea of the interval between the departure from Le Guichet (V, 15) and the arrival at the Royaulme de Quinte Essence (V, 19). It is impossible, consequently, to determine with any great precision how long the journey both ways lasted, but, as closely as it can be approximated, the actual time spent in *sailing* between Thalasse and the Bottle varies between about thirty-five and forty days. If we add to that the time spent on the various islands where the travelers landed, the total time of the outward journey cannot well be under fifty days. Furthermore, Pantagruel set sail on June 7; on July 29, 1546—fifty-two days later—was held the council of Trent, which Rabelais makes meet in Lantern-land, a very short distance from the Bottle. Now, Pantagruel and his companions, while at sea, hear of this council, and say: ".... si lors y arrivions (*comme facile nous estoit*) voyrions belle honorable, et joyeuse compagnie des Lanternes" (IV, 5), which positively shows that Rabelais planned that the voyage from Thalasse to Utopia should require at the most fifty-two days.

In the second place, it is a fair inference that Rabelais did not allow his expedition to sail on an uncharted sea and discover islands at random, but made a map for his own guidance, indicating on it with painstaking accuracy the various lands Pantagruel should run across, and stop at, and both the time necessary to reach each one and the time spent in each. It is undoubtedly to such a map that allusion is made in IV, 1: "Iceluy [Xenomanes] .... avoit à Gargantua laissé et signé, en sa grande et universelle hydrographie, la route qu'ils tiendroient visitans l'oracle de la Dive Bouteille Bacbuc."

In conception the last three books are fundamentally different from the first two. Rabelais sought, nevertheless, to give his work unity after a fashion. He attempted to do so

(*a*) by choosing a bottle as the symbol of the oracle. This choice very likely was suggested by the copious drinking in the first two books, and the frequent use in them of the word *buveurs;*

(*b*) by making, with only one important exception, the protagonists of Books I and II the protagonists of Books III, IV, and V;

(*c*) by the adoption, in a modified form, as the theme of Book III and the pretext of the voyage to the Dive Bouteille, of one of the episodes he had promised to treat in the 'continuation' to Book II: ".... et là vous verrez comment Panurge fut marié, et cocqu dès le premier mois de ses noces."

What impelled Rabelais once more to resume writing after an interval of eleven years, and what determined the character his new work assumed? Lefranc seems to have answered at least the first question satisfactorily. He shows that the centuries-old Quarrel of the Ladies, which had played such a large part in the literature and the history of ideas of the Middle Ages, after a slumber of a few years had once more been revived and had by 1542 reached a climax which continued for fifteen years.[15] The genesis of this quarrel Joseph Bédier attributes to "ce fond de rancune que l'homme a toujours eu contre la femme."[16]   In *L'Estoire del Graal*[17] the attitude and point of view of medieval times toward woman is pithily and characteristically set forth: ".... deable cose et moult doutable avoit en femme car encontre son grant enging ne peut seus homme durer." Around this theme the medieval writer spun endless tales. Even in the romances, with their idealistic and aristocratic tradition, the gentle sex was frequently treated with anything but gentleness. The theme of the frailty of woman runs through every form of Old French literature, and is especially developed in the fabliaux. Initiated in all probability about 1159 by the fabliau *Richeut*, the quarrel has gone on ever since almost down to our own day,[18] with now and then, however, periods of subsidence. Very acute in the second half of the fifteenth century, it partially subsided in the first years of the sixteenth, but was revived in 1515 by Tiraqueau's *De legibus connubialibus*, which rapidly went through several editions. A third edition appeared in 1524, enlarged by quotations from classical authors, which Rabelais is thought to have helped to collect.[19] It was not until 1542, however, that the quarrel began to reach its climax, with the publication in that year at Lyons of Heroët's *Parfaicte Amye*, "a poem of feminine chivalry." Republished in 1543, from 1544 to 1550 it went through ten editions, and inspired in its favor and against

---

[15] *R. E. R.* II, 1–10, 78–109.

[16] *Les Fabliaux*, 281.

[17] H. Oskar Sommer, *The Vulgate Version of the Arthurian Romances*, I, 183.

[18] T. Branagan, *The Excellency of the Female Character Vindicated* (1808).

[19] Tilley, *Francois Rabelais*, 186 *seq.* Rabelais' copy of Gratien du Pont's *Controversies of the Masculine and Feminine Sexes* (1537) still exists.

it a multitude of compositions.[20]   Lefranc asserts that in the ten years which preceded the Pléiade, the Quarrel was, with the resurrection of Platonism, the outstanding fact in the history of ideas.

In the *Parfaicte Amye* Heroët states the Neoplatonic theory of love current during the Renaissance, and in France in vogue especially at Marguerite de Navarre's court.

There are three essential elements in this theory: Beauty, Goodness, Love. The cornerstone of the theory is Plato's doctrine (*Symposium*, 201D) that earthly love uplifts one to the knowledge of God. The theory assimilates Beauty to the body, and Goodness to the soul (*Parfaicte Amye*, 820). The beauty which shines forth in the body is but a spark of the divine and immortal Beauty (876–878) ; Beauty, accordingly, is also a reflection of the divine Goodness (1380). The soul existed in God before quickening the body, and therefore knew divine Beauty. When it became imprisoned in the body it forgot its former existence and the divine Beauty, except in a few cases, where one soul recognizes another as having previously formed part with it of the divine Beauty. This recognition is Love.

Love is attested to by the intellect, not by the senses (567– 574). The reunion in Love of two souls is accompanied by a divine frenzy, transport, and rapture which cause the lovers to become oblivious of their earthly portion. While their souls— which are the masters—are drinking in that divine joy, their bodies—which are the servants—may partake too of earthly joy. When the souls return to their bodies after their rapture they are no longer cognizant of the joy the latter tasted synchronously with them (593–608).

---

[20] Ferdinand Gohin, *Antoine Heroët, Oeuvres poétiques* (Paris, 1909), in the Notice biographique, p. 20, says: "C'est le contraire qui est vrai: La *Parfaicte Amye* est une réponse a l'*Amie de Court*, et le point de départ de ce débat fut la publication et la vogue du *Courtisan*, ouvrage de l'Italien Balthasar Castiglione." The *Amie de Court* of La Borderie, an antifeminist contribution to the Quarrel, was published in 1541.

In her celebrated definition of the perfect lover (*Heptam-eron*, 19), Marguerite calls this Beauty and Goodness the soul's Sovereign Good, and its desire to attain to this Sovereign Good is Love:

.... Car l'ame qui n'est créée que pour retourner à son souverain bien, ne fait tant qu'elle est dedans ce corps que désirer y parvenir. Mais à cause que les sens par lesquels elle en peut avoir nouvelles, sont obscurs et charnels par le péché du premier père, ne luy peuvent monstrer que les choses visibles plus approchantes de la perfection, après quoi l'ame court, cuidans trouver en une beaulté extérieure, en une grace visible et aux vertus morales, la souveraine beaulté, grace, et vertu.

In brief, Love, according to the Neoplatonists, may be defined succinctly in these terms: Love is the soul's effort to realize the Beauty and Goodness it intuitively remembers.

The quarrel eventually involved almost all the writers of the time. In this controversy Rabelais could not remain a passive onlooker. There could be no doubt on which side would be found the man who had dismissed the death of Grandgousier's wife with the cynical words, "Bien penser m'en soucie ni d'elle ni d'autre femme que soit." The last three books of Rabelais, it is clear, are an attack on the views on woman and love upheld by Marguerite and her circle. In order to challenge and fix the attention of his opponents, and to join the issue squarely, he addresses their leader in a *dixain* which he prefixes to the third book, entitled "François Rabelais à l'esprit de la Royne de Navarre":

Esprit abstraict, ravy, et ecstatic,
Qui, fréquentant les cieulx, ton origine,

.   .   .   .   .   .

Voudrois tu point faire quelque sortie
De ton manoir divin, perpetuel,
Et ça bas voir une tierce partie
Des *Faicts* joyeux *du bon Pantagruel?*

If there was anything to cause surprise at all it was the ultimate nature of his thesis and the learning, eloquence, and extraordinary vigor with which he developed it. He reduced the question to its final term: Can a woman remain faithful to her husband,

and in consequence, should a man marry? Rabelais expresses what is without doubt his own opinion of women in the words he attributes to Rondibilis:

Quand je dis femme, je dis un sexe tant fragil, tant variable, tant muable, tant inconstant et imparfaict, que nature me semble (parlant en tout honneur et révérence) s'estre esgarrée de ce bon sens par lequel elle avoit créé et formé toutes choses, quand elle a basty la femme (III, 32).

Such a question, however, cannot be answered dogmatically. This knowledge—like all knowledge really worth having—is purchased through one's own experience. To this effect is the reply of the Divine Bottle, to whom appeal is made for an answer after philosopher and fool, priest and layman, scientist and ordinary man had failed to reply convincingly as well as categorically.

To the solution of this problem, then, the quest of the Divine Bottle addresses itself. But in its course Rabelais somewhat loses sight of his original thesis, and the quest of the Bottle becomes broadened and generalized in the end into a Quest after the Sovereign Good.

The Sovereign Good of the Neoplatonists consists, as we have just seen, in the attainment of Beauty and Goodness through Love; the Sovereign Good of the Grail-quest romances, we shall see,[21] consists in communion with God. In the second part of his work Rabelais definitely reacts against these two aspects of the same mystical conception, and proposes a novel notion of the Sovereign Good, which he makes consist in the pursuit of Knowledge and the cultivation of Wisdom and Truth.

---

[21] See in chapter 5, What the Quest of the Holy Grail is, the last paragraph of the same chapter, and Conclusions.

CHAPTER IV

THE FRAMEWORK OF BOOKS I AND II COMPARED
WITH THAT OF A TYPICAL ROMANCE

I

PRELIMINARY REMARKS

Concerning the form in which Rabelais chose to cast his work, W. F. Smith says: "The framework of the book was in a way supplied by the Romances and Legends of Chivalry and Stories of Giants which were so much in vogue at the time, such as *Amadis de Gaule, Les quatre fils Aymon, Fierabras, Huon de Bordeaux,* and a host of others."[1]

This passage is chosen for citation as representative of the views of those scholars who see in Rabelais' five books an imitation of the so-called Romances of Chivalry, for the reason that it illustrates unusually well the confusion which prevails in the classification of the *rifacimenti* of the older epics and romances printed in the times of Rabelais. Smith probably does not mean to differentiate between the Romances and Legends of Chivalry, by which terms, with Tilley and Besch and many others, he designates such romances as *Fierabras, Les quatre fils Aymon,* and *Huon de Bordeaux,* and presumably the Arthurian Romances; and by Stories of Giants he doubtless alludes to such works as the *Grandes Chroniques, Le Disciple de Pantagruel,* and the *Morgante.* The classification under "Romances of Chivalry" of the prose adaptations of the old epics and romances printed in general between 1478 and 1550 is inherently faulty, and for the purposes of this study misleading. Accordingly it becomes necessary to suggest *in limine* a new classification.

---

[1] *The Works of Rabelais Translated in English,* Introduction, p. 43.

This classification will not be found to differ materially from that of Gaston Paris. Paris, it will be recalled, observed the following classification of early French narrative poetry:[2]

The Epic. In it the chief personage is placed in such a position that the basic qualities of his character stand out clearly. Usually the mainspring of the actions of the epic hero is *desmesure.* The *matière* of the epic is French.

The Romance. Of this *genre* there are three types: (*a*) Romances of Antiquity, whose *matière* is classical; (*b*) Arthurian Romances (*romans bretons*); (*c*) Romances of Adventure.[3] In the Arthurian Romance, the *matière,* originally Celtic, became French (*francisée*) with Chrétien de Troyes, and its treatment and that of the hero is idealistic. In it the mainsprings of action are chivalry and love, with love subordinate and inciting to chivalry.[4] In the Romance of Adventure, the *matière* was originally Byzantine or Oriental and afterwards French. Its treatment is realistic, that of the personages psychological. Love is the main element and chivalry is incidental.[5]

Now, in the adaptations of the old epics and romances published up to 1553, as has already been pointed out (chap. 2), the epic often became contaminated with the romance. In such cases of contamination—of which *Ogier le Danois* is a good example—it was sought by the addition to the original story of certain peculiarities of form and matter proper to the romance more or less to dress up the epic in the garb of the romance. These hybrids have generally been called, along with the Arthurian Romances, Romances of Chivalry. This designation, it is at

---

[2] *La Littérature française au moyen âge* (ed. 2, 1913). On the epic and its divisions see §§ 48, 52, 89, 90, 91, 92; on the romance and its divisions see §§ 95, 96, 97, 102.

[3] This classification is an extension of Jean Bodel's, found in the oft-quoted lines from his *Chanson des Saisnes:*

Ne sont que trois materes a nul home entendant,
De France et de Bretaingne et de Rome la grant,
Et de ces trois materes nia nule semblant.

[4] See *Erec,* 2463–2506 for a statement of this doctrine.

[5] C. V. Langlois, *La Vie française au treizième siècle d'après dix romans d'aventure,* is interesting in this connection.

once evident, is not a very happy one: in the first place, it confuses two different types of *matière,* and in the second it gives a wrong idea of those adaptations and late imitations of the epic which suffered little or no contamination in form or in matter with the romance. Examples of these are *Les quatre fils Aymon* and *Fierabras.*

Accordingly, for the present study, the following classification is suggested:

Gest Romances,[6] which would include all the adaptations of the ancient *matière de France* and the later imitations of it, like the *Mabrian,* howsoever closely or remotely related they may be in *form* to the romance proper.

Romances of Antiquity. Few of these were adapted and published in Rabelais' time, and they left no impress on his work.

Romances of Chivalry, which would include all the adaptations of the old Arthurian Romances—*matière de Bretagne*—and their later imitations, like *Le petit Artus de Bretagne.*

Romances of Adventure, which would agree with the classification generally accepted (p. 177).... It may be said that though many romances of this type were adapted and published in Rabelais' day their influence on his work was nil. Consequently they, as well as the Romances of Antiquity, will receive no further attention here.[7]

This brings us to a consideration of the essential *formal* difference between the epic and the romance. It might be said with a fair degree of accuracy that the *Iliad* is an epic, the *Odyssey* a romance, while the *Aeneid* is a romantic epic, as it shows characteristics of both forms. In the epic the action concerns

---

[6] *Romans de geste.*

[7] Paris calls such a romance as *Mélusine,* and Firmin-Didot such romances as *Valentin et Orson* and *Robert le Diable, romans d'aventure.* They are not *Schicksal* or *fate* romances, but a mixture of the various types. See chap. 2, note 3, for a definition. As has already been said, there has not yet appeared a comprehensive and satisfactory classification of the various types of romances, and such a one is probably impossible and unnecessary. *Le petit Jehan de Saintré* may be instanced as one of the later *romans d'aventure.* It is, as it were, a manual of chivalry and courtly love.

itself with the deeds of a hero or a group of heroes, which are
almost exclusively warlike, and are projected on a conflict
between clans or tribes or nations constituting the background
of the epic.   The action of the epic revolves in general within
the orbit of this conflict.   In the romance, on the contrary, the
personages are shown as going through a series of episodic adventures (often consisting of many incidents) usually unrelated one
with another; frequently there is no background for the deeds
and adventures of the hero,[8] and such background as there may
be is oftener than not fragmentary and devoid of logical connection.   In the *Odyssey* the background against which the
adventures of Ulysses are projected is the ocean; in the French
romances it is a complex of conventions, some literary, some
social, some political, some religious.   Discussion of the background of the romance forms an integral part of this chapter,
and this topic will be treated at greater length in the sequel.

Addressing ourselves more specifically to the French epic and
romance, we find good contrasting characterizations of them in
the *Histoire littéraire de la France*.   With regard to the epic,
Paulin Paris says:

La Chanson de geste devait être et fut effectivement avant tout un poème
guerrier. Les sentiments délicats de la vie paisible n'y tiennent qu'une
place étroite et accidentelle; les actions intrépides, les grands effets de la
force corporelle, les lâches trahisons, les généreux dévouements, les calam-
ités ou les victoires décisives, eurent le privilège d'y saisir et d'y captiver
l'attention des auditeurs.[9]

And respecting the romance Gaston Paris expresses himself in
these words:

Ils se divisent en deux classes, les romans biographiques et les romans
épisodiques. Les premiers prennent un héros depuis sa naissance, ou au
moins depuis son apparition à la cour d'Arthur où se présente à lui l'aventure qui doit faire le principal sujet du roman, et nous racontent plus ou
moins longuement ses prouesses, qui aboutissent à son mariage. Les romans

---

[8] The *matière* of the epic often is incorporated in the romance, when a
struggle between armies forms the background for the deeds of the hero.
On the subject of transition in content from epic to romance, see N. E.
Griffin, *Publications of the Modern Language Association of America*,
XXXVIII, No. 1, 50–70.

[9] XXII, 259.

épisodiques, au contraire, généralement plus brefs, nous retracent un épisode, mais souvent composé de beaucoup d'aventures enchevêtrées les unes dans les autres, de la vie d'un héros célèbre.[10]

The romance, then, differs from the epic both in *matière* and in form. In the typical biographical romance the main thread of the narrative will be found to fall under the following divisions: Prologue, Ancestry of the hero, his Youth and Education, his Exploits, his Marriage.[11] Of all these parts the epic exhibits only the Exploits of its hero.[12]

The epic, of course, is the direct ancestor of the romance. The romance might accurately enough be said to correspond, on its *formal* side, to the epic family. The epic family originated in some such manner: as the number of epic poems increased the *jongleurs* arranged them in families, each headed by the name of an ancestor; the 'hub' of the family was its earliest epic, usually a poem brief enough to be capable of being concluded in a single recitation, and exhibiting the hero in the maturity of his power. The family grew in two ways: first, an independent poem presented under the guise of a 'preface' the youth of the hero and his early exploits—*enfances*—or perhaps his 'ancestry,' recounting the fortunes of his forbears; sequels followed describing additional exploits of the hero[13] or of his descendants or collaterals. The epic family, accordingly, exhibits from the point of view of the romance structure the following phases, in logical sequence: Ancestry, Youth, and Exploits, with certain other phases, such as Marriage, implied.

---

[10] XXX, 14.

[11] To these might be added the hero's Birth and his Appareling, were it not that they are of minor importance and are sketchily given when not altogether omitted.

[12] Wolfram's *Parzival* and *Robert le Diable*, among others, show all the divisions. Many romances omit one or more of them. The *Lancelot* omits Marriage, for instance, and *Erec* and *Clériadus et Méliadice* (1495) omit all but Exploits and Marriage.

[13] Compare, however, the growth of the Perceval cycle of romances; also the evolution of *Amadis de Gaula*, James Fitzmaurice-Kelly, *Littérature espagnol* (1913), 158–162, 218, and Pascual de Gayangos, "Discurso preliminar," *Biblioteca de autores españoles*, XL.

The authors of romances synthetized the *form* of the epic family and within a single poem presented (with considerable abbreviation, naturally, of the less essential parts) the various phases of the hero's activities which previously had required as many different poems for presentation. With this alteration in form there went an associated change in *matière*:[14] the *matière* of the epic purports to be historical and national, the *matière* of the romance is legendary and folkloristic. In the Old French epics the central personages are usually Charlemagne and his twelve peers, all in arms to deliver France and Europe from the Saracens; in the romances the central personage is Arthur, whose knights devote their lives to knightly deeds and to the quest of the Holy Grail.

From these remarks it will be clear that Rabelais' work, as a whole, in its *evolution* partakes of the nature of the epic, and in its *form*, of the nature of the romance. The five books grew as the epic family did: first, the second book—the *Pantagruel*—created the hero; the success of the *Pantagruel*, in the second place, suggested the *Gargantua*—the first book—which embodies the Ancestry phase; thirdly, the further exploits of the hero were related—Books III, IV, V. In form, both the *Pantagruel* and the *Gargantua* exhibit the architectonics of the Arthurian Romance. In the *Pantagruel* we find the following divisions: Prologue, Ancestry, Youth and Education, Exploits; and in the *Gargantua*, Prologue, Youth and Education, Exploits, and, inferentially, Marriage.

---

[14] See Maurice Wilmotte, *L'Evolution du roman français aux environs de 1150* (Bouillon, Paris, 1913).

II

GENERAL OUTLINE OF THE STORY

The treatment of this division of the present chapter involves a discussion of the Old French romance on its formal side, i.e., a discussion of its framework.

§ 1.   THE PROLOGUE

Few types of medieval French compositions were without their prologue. Usually the prologue invites the reader to tarry and promises him "une joyeuse histoire,"[15] "gentement or-donée,"[16] or "belles aventures,"[17] or the story related may be "le meilleur conte . . . . qui soit contez an cort real.'"[18] In the course of time the tone of the prologue degenerated, and the reader was enticed in shameless terms.

Approchez, approchez [shouts the adapter of the incunabular *Maugis d'Aigremont*[19] to his audience], nous possédons dans nos magasins de quoi satisfaire les goûts les plus variés et les plus difficiles; nous avons un vaste assortiment de fées, d'enchanteurs, de chevaliers, de nains, de géants, de batailles, de tournois, de coup d'épées, de coups de lance, de contes d'amour, de conquêtes et de beaux faits d'armes, de miracles et de merveilles de toutes sortes, de rois et d'empereurs, de reines et de princesses belles comme le jour, tout revu, corrigé, augmenté, et orné de belles figures. Approchez.

This side-show puff left its traces in Rabelais. Not a single one of his six prologues but begins with some adjuration or an-other to his reader, while the Prologue de l'auteur, Book IV, strikes exactly the tone of the *Maugis*. "Gens de bien," shouts Rebelais, simulating the 'barker," "Dieu vous saulve et gard! Où estes vous? Attendez que je chausse mes lunettes . . . . Ha, ha! Bien et beau s'en va quaresme! Je vous voy . . . ."

---

[15] *Jehan de Paris.*

[16] *Beaudouin de Sebourc.*

[17] *Le Chevalier au Papegau.*

[18] *Li Contes del Graal.*

[19] Gautier, *Les Epopées françaises*, ed. 2, II, 612, *seq.* See also the pro-logue of the *Helyas* (*Godefroy de Bouillon*, 1504), and *Perceforest*, 1531.

But the prologue was usually more serious and dignified, especially in the earlier romances. Chrétien de Troyes uses it more than once as a vehicle to express his literary doctrine. In his prologues he frequently mentions the *sans* and *matiere* of which his works are compounded. By *sans* he means the *sciance* or *sapiance* with which one is primitively endowed as a poet. By using his *sans* properly the poet imparts to his work a "signification" proceeding from the "interpretation" to be placed on his *matiere*, according as he has moulded his *matiere*. Accordingly, in the eyes of Chrétien, *sans* might mean the *knowledge* or inspiration of the poet and the interpretation to be put on his text. In the later medieval ages, with Dante for example, this doctrine was further elaborated, and crystallized finally into the four "significations" assigned to poetry: the literal, the allegorical, the moral or philosophical, the anagogic or mystic.[20]

This more sober function of the prologue, too, left its echo in Rabelais:

.... faut auvrir le livre [he warns the reader in the Prologue of the *Gargantua*], et soigneusement peser ce qui est deduict. Lors cognoistrez que la drogue dedans contenue est bien d'aultre valeur que ne promettait la boite: c'est à dire que les *matieres* icy traictées ne sont tant folastres comme le tiltre au dessus pretendoit.

Et posé le cas qu'au *sens literal* vous trouvez *matieres* assez joyeuses et bien correspondentes au nom, toutesfois pas demeurer là ne faut comme au chant des sirenes; ains à *plus hault sens* interpreter ce que par aventure cuidiez dict en gaieté de coeur.

Puis, par curieuse leçon et meditation frequente, rompre l'os et subcer la substantifique *mouelle* .... avec espoir certain d'estre faicts escors et preux à ladicte lecture, car en icelle bien aultre goust trouverez et *doctrine plus absconse*, laquelle vous revelera de tres haults sacrements et mysteres horrifiques, tant en ce qui concerne nostre religion que aussi l'estat politiq et vie oeconomique.

In this prologue Rabelais has in contemplation, besides the literal meaning of his writings, now and then an allegorical[21]

---

20 Wm. A. Nitze, *Rom.* XLIV, 14.

21 See *Orlando innamorato*, XXV, 6, and XXXIV 2–3, where Berni admonishes his reader in the same manner as Rabelais.

and more frequently a philosophical meaning also.[22]   In claiming this manifold "signification" for his work, Rabelais harks back to a long and well-established medieval tradition which nevertheless he ridicules in the same prologue:

> Croyez-vous en vostre foy qu'oncques Homere escrivant l'*Iliade* et l'*Odyssée* pensast es allegories lesquelles de luy ont calfreté Plutarche, Heraclides Ponticq, Eustatie, Phornute, et ce que d'iceux Politian a desrobé? Si le croyez vous n'approchez ne de pieds ne de mains à mon opinion qui decrete icelles aussi peu avoir esté songées d'Homere que d'Ovide en ses *Metamorphoses* les sacrements de l'Evangile....

§ 2. ANCESTRY

In *Cligès* about half of the poem is given over to an account of the life and deeds of Alexandre, the hero's father.   Hence *Cligès* is, so to say, a double romance.   It is very unusual to find so much space devoted to the lineage of the hero; much more frequently this phase is disposed of in one chapter, or in two or three at the most.   The recital of the hero's ancestry need not confine itself to his direct forbears.   In the *Perlesvaus* it concerns itself quite as much with Perceval's collateral kin: it is given fully, both on his mother's side and on his father's, and his twelve uncles are carefully listed.[23]   In the *Lancelot* we are told who the father and the mother of Lancelot were, also the names and history of their brother and sister, respectively; the wars the two kings had been compelled to wage against Claudas, a hostile neighbor; the vicissitudes that they experienced in the course of these wars; the treachery of the seneschal of Lancelot's father, Ban, which resulted in the loss of Ban's last stronghold and his consequent death of grief, likewise the death of his brother Bohors; and finally the taking of the veil by Lancelot's mother and his aunt.[24]   In *Le petit Artus de Bretagne* we are

---

[22] See W. F. Smith, *Rabelais in his Writings, passim,* for the significance of the five books.

[23] Charles Potvin, *Perceval le Gallois,* I, 1–3; *Perceval* (1530), chaps. 1–2.

[24] Sommer, III, 1–22; *Lancelot* (1533), first part, ff. 1–5.

given an account of Arthur's father and of his mother, and his lineage is traced back to Lancelot on the paternal side.[25]

In *Pantagruel*—"De l'origine et antiquité du grand Pantagruel"— Rabelais gives the family tree of his giant from the remotest times. Sixty ascendants of Pantagruel are listed in it. He gives as his reason for doing this the universal custom of chronicles; "aussi les auteurs de la Saincte Escriture, comme monseigneur Sant Luc" have done likewise. It is plain from these words, taken in conjunction with the form in which he lists his hero's forbears, that Rabelais is here parodying Biblical genealogies. Of the sixty giant ancestors of Pantagruel, a few are of Rabelais' own invention, one is taken from the Scriptures, one from history, eleven from the French and Italian epics and romances, and the rest from mythology and popular tradition.

§ 3. Youth and Education

The story of the youth of the hero frequently assumes an extensive development in the romances. In the *Lancelot,* for example, this part alone of the romance amounts to what would be a book of average length. The *enfances* of Lancelot covers a period between about his second and his eighteenth year, when he goes to Arthur's court to be knighted .... In a general way, this part of the story adumbrates the character which the hero will be given in the sequel.

Of prime importance in the formative period of the hero's life is his education. In *Le petit Artus de Bretagne* Arthur is "delivered under the governance of a gentle master named Governor," who taught him to play chess and tables. When he was twenty, Governor taught him how to skirmish, taught him the ways of courtesy and gave him moral instruction.[26] At a very tender age Lancelot was given a master "qui lenseigna et

---

[25] Chap. 1, Lord Berners' translation.
[26] Chap. 2.

monstra comment il se tiendrait en maniere de gentilhomme.''[27]
When he was barely out of the cradle his master made for him
a bow and arrows and taught him their use. When he was a
little older he was taught how to kill the birds of the forest and
to shoot hares. When he was grown enough to ride he was
given a steed and costume and taught how to ride cross-country.
Furthermore, he was taught all kinds of games,[28] especially
chess, at all of which he excelled. So much for the physical
side of his education.[29] The Lady of the Lake undertook herself
his moral education. The lessons she inculcated in him and the
manner of their inculcation recall the *chastoiements* of the Middle Ages,[30] one of which, indeed, did find its way into a romance.[31] The Lady explained to Lancelot the origin and purpose

[27] *Lancelot* (1533), first part, f. 10. See Alwin Schultz, *Das höfische
Leben*, I, 156–162, on the education of the nobility in the Middle Ages.
The education of the prince differed from that of the knight in being more
extensive, foreign tongues, among other accomplishments, not being neglected. Generally, reading and writing received scant attention, though
some heroes of romance, Lancelot for example, could both read and write.
It is worth noting that Wolfram von Eschenbach on several occasions
proudly boasts of his inability to do either. Cf. *Galien rethoré*, Troyes
reprint (Garnier, 1723?), chap. 12. In his boyhood Galien is put to school,
until one day he rides to death a horse of his foster-father's, who thereupon
says: ''C'est une grande folie l'envoyer à l'école, car il ressemble bien à
celui qui l'a engendré; il fera en son temps vaillant chevalier. Je vous
promets, ma foi, que jamais il n'étudiera.''

[28] Cf. Rabelais, I, 22, ''Les jeux de Gargantua.''

[29] On the physical education of the youth of the Middle Ages, see
Schultz, I, 162–173; on his warlike education, the first book of *L'Art de
chevalerie*, and of *Li Ahrejance de l'ordre de chevalerie*, vols. 39 and 40,
respectively, of the *Société des anciens textes français*. Léon Gautier, in
La Chevalerie, in the chapter entitled ''L'Enfance du baron,'' presents
interestingly the physical, moral, intellectual, and religious education of the
noble youth of the feudal period.

[30] On the *Chastoiements*, see Petit de Julleville, *Histoire de la langue
et de la littérature française*, II, 185–188. The *chastoiement* is a didactic
composition whose end is moral discipline. ''Le castoiement d'un père à
son fils,'' Barbazan-Méon, II, 39, represents a father who is giving precepts
to his son when the latter is about to leave the parental roof. These precepts are, love and fear of God, love of work, discretion in making friends,
fidelity to obligations, loyalty, continence, humility, fidelity to the king,
and admonitions against raillery, against ambition, and against avarice
and prodigality.

[31] In Robert de Blois' *Beaudous*, when the mother is advising her son
as to his conduct, the opportunity is used to introduce religious and didactic
poems in the romance. One of the interpolations is ''Le Chastoiement des
dames,'' Barbazan-Méon, II, 184.

of the institution of chivalry and the qualities the knight should possess. She described the arms of the knight and their symbolism[32] and upon delivering him over to Arthur's care she gave him her final precepts.

The importance of the youth's education in the romances is attested by the fact that Mélusine *chastoie* each one of her sons as he sets out on his career of adventures.[33] She discourses to them on morals, statecraft, military and religious conduct, and liberality.

As every reader knows, the youth, and especially the education, of Gargantua and Pantagruel constitute an important part of the two books, and receive detailed attention. The first need detain us but briefly—suffice it to say that Pantagruel's physical proportions so delighted his father that he "luy fit faire . . . . une arbaleste pour s'esbattre aprés les oisillons" (II, 5); and that Gargantua "passa les trois jusques à cinq ans . . . . commes les petits enfants du pays" (I, 2). When Pantagruel was still very young he was sent off "à l'école pour passer son jeune age" (II, 5), and Gargantua was entrusted to the care of Thubal Holoferne "sur la fin de la quinte année." On his university tour, which resembles closely the wanderings of the *scholasticus vagabundus* of the Middle Ages,[34] Pantagruel showed at first an inclination to continue his youthful exploits. At Paris, however, he found a school more to his liking than any he had previously visited, and so he set seriously to work. In this he was encouraged by his father, who addressed to him the celebrated letter (II, 8) which has been called "le chant triomphal de la Renaissance." In this letter, Rabelais sketches the curriculum a gentleman should follow who wishes to become "absolu et parfaict . . . . en tout savoir libéral et honneste."

---

32 Sommer, III, 22; *Lancelot* (1533), first part, ff. 30–31. On the institution of chivalry, its form and spirit, in history and romance, see Roy Temple House, *L'Ordene de chevalerie*, 7–27 (University of Chicago dissertation, 1918).

33 *Mélusine, passim.*

34 See Paul Monroe, *The Autobiography of Thomas Platter* (New York, 1904); also N. H. Clement, "A Note on Panurge," *Romanic Review*, XV, 285–295.

These brief indications he later amplified in the chapters dealing with Gargantua's education (I, 24–25).   Gargantua, on his arrival at Paris, must needs have in his turn an exploit or two to his credit and give the people of the capital, who are "tant sot, tant badaut, et tant inepte de nature," a striking manifestation of his prowess.   He carries off, accordingly, the bells of Notre Dame.   After being given an opportunity to witness at the Sorbonne the older system of education, which "l'avait rendu tant fat, niays et ignorant," he is "institued in letters" by Ponocrates in quite a different manner.   His tutor aimed to make his education universal.   Equal attention was paid to his physical and his intellectual training, and his moral and religious education was in no wise neglected.   It is noteworthy that at dinner[35] Ponocrates had read to him "quelque histoire plaisante des anciennes prouesses"— the romances — and that much time was devoted to his instruction in "l'art de chevalerie," when, armed *cap à pie,* he was trained in the use of lance, battle-ax, sword, and dagger, the weapons of the heroes of epic and romance.[36]

In brief, in the education which Rabelais was recommending to the young gentleman of the Renaissance he kept constantly in mind the ideal of the old Roman, *mens sana in corpore sano*— that is, a classical, Graeco-Roman ideal.

§ 4.   Exploits and Marriage

It need scarcely be said that the recital of the deeds of valor of the hero constitutes by far the chief part of the romance, and invariably receives a length of treatment commensurate with its importance.   In the greater number of the romances the hero's

---

[35] See *Las siete Partidas* of Alphonso the Wise, Book II, tit. 21, law 20, for the rules governing the entertainment of nobles during meals in medieval Spain.   To instill in the hearers a warlike spirit, *cantares de gesta* were read to them, and their conversation was restricted to *fechas darmas.*

[36] In the letter of Gargantua to Pantagruel, Rabelais, echoing the *Orl. fur.* IX, 18–29, says that firearms were invented "par suggestion diabolique," the implication being that their invention caused the decay of chivalry.

exploits are interwoven with a love story which usually ends in marriage.[37]   In Rabelais there is no heroine, an omission traceable to his contemptuous attitude toward women, and of a love story there is only an inkling.   In II, 23, we learn that when Pantagruel was about to sail for Utopia he received a letter from a lady of Paris whom ''he had kept and entertained for a good space.''   In the other books there is not even so much as that.   In this almost total exclusion of woman, Rabelais' work calls to mind the Gest Romances rather than the Arthurian Romances.

At first sight, too, very much like that of the Gest Romances is Rabelais' treatment of the exploits of his heroes, especially in the *Gargantua,* which unfold themselves on the background of the Picrocholine and Dipsodic wars. [38]   This resemblance is very largely superficial, however, as is readily apparent from the fact that these two conflicts, far from being of primary importance in the structure of the story, as they are in the Gest Romances, are merely episodic, and as episodes have innumerable counterparts in the Arthurian Romances.   Indeed, it is in this relegation of warfare from a position of main to one of merely episodic interest—by which it was enabled to assume characteristics that brought it into broader contact with life—that the romance shows a distinct technical, aesthetic, and ethical advance over the epic.   With these remarks further consideration of the exploits of the hero will be deferred until the topic of War in the Romances is taken up below.

---

[37] In the *Lancelot* naturally there is no marriage, though its place is in a great measure taken by the love subsisting between Lancelot and Guenevere.   Other romances might be cited in this connection.

[38] The combat between Pantagruel and Loupgarou has sufficient points of resemblance with that between Oliver and Fierabras in the *Fierabras* to raise a strong presumption that Rabelais was here directly inspired by this Gest Romance.

III

SPECIFIC RESEMBLANCES OF DETAIL BETWEEN RABELAIS AND THE ROMANCES

§ 1. BACKGROUND OF THE ROMANCE

The discussion of this division of the present chapter involves a discussion of the background of the romance. This background, as already said, is complex, and variable. In an episodic romance, like *Erec,* or *La mule sans frein,* it is scarcely perceptible.; in a biographical romance, like *Lancelot du Lac,* it is highly elaborated. The commonest, though not exclusive or essential, constituent elements of the background of the typical romance are:

(*a*) Chivalric customs, and knightly qualities of the hero

(*b*) Investitures

(*c*) Foundations

(*d*) Authentications

(*e*) Political organization of the country

(*f*) Central position of Arthur[39]

(a) Chivalric customs and knightly qualities of the hero—

In *Cligès*[40] we learn that a king's son on his travels should be accompanied by vassals (1275, 1483) .... While it is not customary for a king to engage in errantry, his sons always do

---

[39] These topics are chosen not only because they are the most characteristic ones, but also because they are the ones that Rabelais especially kept before him in constructing the background of his romance; and as the writer's intention is merely to establish a basis of comparison, they will be very briefly treated.

[40] Cf. *Jehan de Paris* for the retinue that accompanied Jehan to Spain. In the *Nibelungenlied* (strophe 60) twelve warriors accompanied Siegfried to the land of the Burgundians. See also P. Guilhiermoz, *Essai sur l'origine de la noblesse en France,* p. 424 and note 12.

so[41].... The accouterment of the knight-errant consists of a
horse and weapons—shield, lance, sword, though on occasion
other weapons may be used, as the battle-ax in battle. Of his
armor, the helmet and the hauberk are the parts more frequently
mentioned.[42].... It is the knight's privilege, while in quest of
adventures, to stop at any castle or other habitation, and claim
hospitality for the night.[43] This custom has an extension: one
lord may pay a visit to another in a purely social way, or under
pretext of soliciting his help in any cause. During such visits
the exchange of presents is not unusual.[44] The giving of presents
is a manifestation of a king's largess, one of his essential attributes, for the lack of which he may be severely censured.[45]

Heralds and messengers play a not unimportant rôle in the
romances. One of the functions of the latter is to bring news
of an irruption of the enemy,[46] while a herald may be dis-
patched to the enemy's camp, as in *Le petit Artus de Bretagne*
(chap. 103), in order to inquire the reason of such an invasion,
and to protest against it.[47]

In the romances, the conquered king or the vanquished
knight, if he would escape death, must yield himself to the victor,
who has the disposal of him, and customarily imposes upon him a
punishment considered adequate to the offence. The usual pen-
alty is for the vanquished knight to present himself as a testi-
monial of his conqueror's prowess to a person the latter designates; but not infrequently the victor exercises his privilege of

---

[41] In the *Chevalier au papegau*, however, Arthur sets out in quest of
adventures immediately after his coronation. Contrast in the *Lancelot* the
aloofness of Arthur and the errantry of his nephews Gawain, Agravain, and
Gareth, all sons of a king; or better still, note the contrast between the
activities of Galehaut and Lancelot.

[42] See Schultz, II, 11–95, on medieval arms and armor; and pp. 132–133
for the weapons used in jousting.

[43] On the hospitality of the Middle Ages, see Schultz, I, 518–523.

[44] See Schultz, Index under *Geschenke*. At I, 637, Schultz discusses the
exchange of presents between host and guest.

[45] *Erec*, 2060.

[46] Sommer, III, 128, 210, 394, etc.; *Lancelot* (1533), first part, ff. 33,
110, etc.

[47] On messengers in the Middle Ages, see Schultz, I, 175–178.

disposing of his opponent by abridging in some way or another his liberty of action.[48]

Probably the most striking of romance customs is that of holding consultations. These are ordinarily called for the purpose of interpreting dreams, though any portent may form their subject. In the *Lancelot* there are two very interesting illustrations of this custom. One of them is the council of wise men whom Galehaut summoned to explain a dream which presaged his coming death.[49] Indicative of the importance of this custom is the space devoted to such a convocation: the deliberations and explanations of the wise men on this occasion would fill about thirty-five pages of an ordinary book. In illustration, a consultation held at Arthur's behest may be instanced. The king dreamt that his hair and beard had fallen out, and two nights later he dreamt that his fingers had dropped off. He summoned his clergy and wise men to interpret these dreams. The clerks deliberated during nine days. After several adjournments, and threats from the king, they gave their interpretation: he would lose all earthly honor, and those in whom he most trusted would fail him against their own will.[50]

The essential knightly qualities that we find associated with these chivalric customs are valor, liberality, courtesy, and amiability.[51]

(b) Investitures—

The genesis of the customs of chivalry is undoubtedly to be traced to the social conventions of the period, while the knightly qualities of the hero are none other than those that have dis-

---

[48] *Lancelot* (1533), first part, f. 82; second part, f. 19, etc., etc.

[49] Sommer, IV, 19–34; *Lancelot* (1533), first part, ff. 120–124.

[50] Sommer, III, 199 *seq; Lancelot* (1533), first part, f. 51. Cf. *Merlin* (1498), first part, ff. 20–22, for the consultation ordered by Vortigern in order to explain why his castle fell several times successively into ruins.

[51] Sommer, III, 30, *passim* in the romances. *Merlin* (1498), first part, ff. 69, 76, offers good illustrations of largess.

tinguished the gentleman of all countries and times. Similarly the investitures[52] which are so common in the romances have their origin in the political and legal organization of feudal society, and correspond exactly to its enfeoffments. The romances are so replete with cases of investiture that it would be otiose to give illustrations.[53]

(c) Foundations[54]

As investitures are a reflection of the politico-legal organization of feudal society, so pious foundations mirror the religious customs of the times, when king, baron, or vavasor compounded his sins, or expressed his gratitude for a signal mercy shown, by founding or endowing a chapel, church, or monastery.[55] Examples of foundations also are countless in the romances, and accordingly require no special emphasis here.[56]

(d) Authentications

The medieval story teller invariably felt the necessity of accrediting his narrative, redundant with wonders as it usually was, and this he sought to do by connecting it with reality or a pseudo-reality. This literary convention assumes many forms. Two of the commonest consist in assigning a definite source,

---

[52] On forms of investiture in Middle Ages consult, under that word, P. A. Chéruel, *Dictionnaire des institutions, moeurs, et coutumes du moyen âge.*

[53] *Le petit Artus de Bretagne,* chap. 39; *Lancelot* (1533), third part, f. 53.

[54] On this topic and the preceding one, see Lavisse, *Histoire de France,* II, part 2, Book I, chap. 1 *passim* (Le régime féodal). This chapter gives an excellent panoramic view of life during the early feudal period.

[55] For the wide prevalence of the custom of founding and endowing churches, monasteries, etc., during the Middle Ages, see *La France monastique,* I, which gives a list of such foundations with names and dates. For a typical example of the *occasion* of a foundation, see in the first chapter of the *Chronicon Monasterii de Bello* the story of the founding of Battle Abbey by William the Conqueror, after the battle of Hastings.

[56] Sommer, V, 144–145; II, 249–250, etc. *L'hystoire du Saint Graal* (1516), f. 101, etc.

usually imaginary, to the narrative,[57] and in linking some of
its incidents in a special manner with the localities in which they
transpired. For instance, "Le mont au chat" is so called
because on it Arthur slew the "cat-monster";[58] and the Ford
of Blood at Arestuel was thus named owing to the great slaugh-
ter Arthur made there of the Saxons.[59] This literary practice
passed into the popular romances and was given an extension
verging on the grotesque.[60]

(e) Political organization—

In the romances the land is divided into an innumerable
number of smaller kingdoms, each having its ruler, who may
be independent or tributary to an overlord. Between these
rulers there subsists perpetual war, chiefly between Arthur
and the rest. These wars often are scarcely more than free-
booting expeditions whose chief aim is conquest, devastation,
and pillage. The pretext not seldom is frivolous. In illustration, in the *Perlesvaus*, King Madeglant wars upon Arthur
because he spurned the love of Jandree, the former's sister.
They are miniature wars in many cases, as is evidenced by the
fact that Lancelot is sent against Madeglant with only forty
knights and destroys him with all his force. (Cf. *L'hystoire du
Saint Graal*, 1516, f. 192).

The case of Galehaut demands special stress in this connection, as he very likely suggested to Rabelais the character of

---

[57] In *Le Roman du Renart* the reason is given for invoking an authority
or source. Regarding the warfare between Renart and Ysengrin, we are
told:
> Si je ne le trovasse el livre,
> Je tenisse celuy por ivre
> Qui dite eust tele aventure;
> Mes l'en doit croire l'escripture.
> *A desenor muert a bon droit*
> *Qui n'aime livre ne ne croit.*

See also *P M L A*, XXXVIII, No. 1, at p. 61.

[58] Paulin Paris, *Les Romans de la Table Ronde*, II, 362. *Perceforest*
(1531) offers profuse illustrations of this practice.

[59] Sommer, III, 408; *L'hystoire du Saint Graal* (1516), f. 103, etc.

[60] See p. 162 for examples in the *Pantagruel*.

Picrochole.   Galehaut, upon assuming his kingship, conceived
the project, he tells Lancelot, of conquering the whole world.
Up to the time he attacked Arthur, who was saved only by Lancelot's intervention, he had already vanquished thirty kings.[61]
Now, Galehaut certainly did produce a marked impression on
Rabelais, who mentions him twice, and Estrangore, one of his
tributary kingdoms, once.   There can be little doubt, when we
recall Rabelais' genius for adaptation and amplification, that
the prototype of the Picrocholine War is to be sought in the
conflict between Galehaut and Arthur,[62] expanded with details
drawn from Plutarch's *Life of Pyrrhus,* and that Picrochole's
dream of universal conquest is a humorously exaggerated copy
of the ambitious projects of the romance king.[63]

(f) Position of Arthur in the Romances—

As we have already seen, in the romances a king might not
engage in *chevalerie,* or knight-errantry.   He could, of course,
in war assume his part in the conflict; or he might properly
achieve an adventure that fortuitously presented itself to him;[64]
or he might participate in tournaments.   This aloofness of a
king from the ordinary pursuits of knighthood is one of the
well-defined literary conventions of the romance, as we may
gather from this incident.   In the *Lancelot,* Bohors emphatically
refuses to accept at the hands of Lancelot investiture with the
kingdom of Gannes, ''car sitost comme j'averoi roiaume il me
convendra lessier tote chevalerie, *ou je veuille ou non;* et c'est
nulle honor a moi ne a vous.   Et certes, plus averoi-je d'onor
se j'estoie povre homme bon chevalier, que je n'aroie riche rois

[61] Sommer, III, 201; *Lancelot* (1533), first part, ff. 51, 114.   For
Italian echoes, see Berni, XXX, 71; Bojardo, Book I, XX, 44–45, Book II,
I; *Morgante maggiore,* XXV, 194.

[62] Cf. *Parzival,* XV, 582–630, Weston's translation, for the conquests
of Parzival and Feirefis.   Universal conquest is a *motif* in several romances.

[63] Anything here said, of course, is not exclusive of M. Lefranc's views—
which I accept as demonstrated—concerning the dispute between Rabelais'
father and Gaucher de Sainte Marthe and its relationship with the *matière*
of the Picrocholine War.

[64] Paulin Paris, II, 344–350.

recreant.''[65] We find accordingly that although Arthur's court is the center whence the knights of the Round Table set forth in all directions in their quest of adventures, he himself does not share in the adventures of errantry; he constitutes, from the point of view of literary function, merely the keystone that holds together the romance edifice.

§ 2.   WAR IN THE ROMANCES

So much for the romance background. Projected on it are the exploits of the hero, which may be presented under two aspects: under that of a knight engaged in errantry, and running through the gamut of conventional adventures—the avenging of a wronged person, the rescue of an imprisoned knight or maiden, the dissipation of the enchantments or evil customs of a castle, the jousting with every knight met on the road, deeds of valor at a tourney, all or any of them being interwoven in a measure with some love story or intrigue; and secondly, under the aspect of the deeds of the hero in time of war. This second and less important phase of the knightly activities of the romançe hero, it has already been pointed out, is an epic characteristic retained in the evolution of the epic into the romance. It is, however, the only one which presently interests us.

In a general way, in the romances, the 'movement' of a war shows the following characteristics: an irruption of a king with his hosts into the territory of another; the arrival of a messenger announcing the news; the summoning of his vassals by the aggrieved prince; his taking the field with his forces; the battle or a siege.[66]

It would be idle to attempt to differentiate between the epic battle and the romance battle. On the one hand, both conform

---

[65] Paulin Paris, V, 323. However, in the *Lancelot* (1533), third part, f. 144, Lancelot invests Bohors with the kingdom of Benoic, and Lyonel with the kingdom of Gannes, and neither refuses.

[66] Sommer, III, 210, 394; *Lancelot* (1533), first part, f. 54; *Le petit Artus de Bretagne* chaps. 88–89; *L'hystoire du Saint Graal* (1516), ff. 21–30, offer typical examples of romance wars.

more or less to the manner of fighting employed in those days; on
the other, the literary function of both is to supply a background
for the exploits of the heroes. The only clear distinction between
the two is the one that already has been made: in the typical
epic, or in the Gest Romance directly derived from it, war and
battles constitute an element of primary importance—a *sine qua
non* of the exploits of the hero—whereas in the Arthurian Romances they are merely episodic and of minor importance.

§ 3.   BACKGROUND IN RABELAIS

In the romances the background gives, to a considerable
degree, a picture of feudal society and its organization, and of
feudal private life. Rabelais was, in his turn, careful to con-
struct a similar society in his first two books, but more particularly in the *Gargantua,* and to develop within its frame the
story of his giants. The background of Rabelais' romance is
strictly analogous with that of the Arthurian Romance.

(a₁) Chivalric customs and knightly qualities—

In the *Pantagruel* it is only implied that Pantagruel, upon
setting out on his university tour, is accompanied by a retinue—
in chapter 5 we learn that his tutor, Epistemon, terminated a
love affair in which he had incontinently become enmeshed in
Avignon; and in chapter 6, when he meets with the Limousin
at Orleans, he is taking a walk after supper with "his companions." In the *Gargantua,* where Rabelais shows himself
more conscious of his models, we are specifically told that Gargantua left his father's court for Paris with a large body of
attendants (chap. 16) . . . . In the Picrocholine and Dipsodic
wars, it is the sons—Gargantua and Pantagruel, respectively—
and not the fathers—Grandgousier and Gargantua—who lead
the armies against the enemy, and, more closely analogous, in
the last two books, it is Pantagruel who sets out in quest of the
Holy Bottle—an undertaking which corresponds closely to the

errantry of the romance hero—while Gargantua remains at home .... The accouterment of the Rabelaisian hero tallies very closely with that of the romance hero. Part of Gargantua's education consists in "la chevalerie et les armes." He goes through the routine of chivalric exercises armed *cap à pie,* his weapons being the ax, the sword, and the dagger (ɪ, 23). When Grandgousier learns of Picrochole's invasion, he calls for his armor, his lance, and his mace (ɪ, 28). Gargantua and his companions, setting out on a reconnoissance of Picrochole's army, harness Frère Jean against his will from head to foot, hang to his side a broadsword, and place a lance in his hands.

The hospitality of the romances finds its reflection in Rabelais.[67] In *Gargantua* 12, three lords independently visit Grandgousier at the same time; and later Grandgousier dismisses Maître Jobelin Bridé, Gargantua's tutor, substituting in his stead Ponocrates, after a visit from the viceroy of Papeligosse, who shows him in Eudemon the superior efficacy of the modern education (ɪ, 15).

Part of Gargantua's apparel is a purse "faite de la couille d'un oriflant," which had been presented to him by Herr Pracontal, consul of Libya (ɪ, 8). Gargantua's mare, too, we recall, is a gift—of the king of Numidia; and Grandgousier shows his magnanimity by giving Toquedillon a beautiful sword when the latter, set at liberty, returns to Picrochole's camp.

Messengers and heralds, likewise, play their part in the Rabelaisian romance. Presumably it is a messenger who announces to Pantagruel the death of his father, and who bears to him the letter of the Parisian lady (ɪɪ, 23) ; it is a messenger who brings to Grandgousier the news of Picrochole's incursion into his domains (ɪ, 28), and Grandgousier sends Ulrich Gallet as his herald to remonstrate against this unfriendly act (ɪ, 30).

Just as the vanquished knight in the romances is at the disposal of his victor, so in the *Pantagruel* Panurge similarly disposes of his prisoner, King Anarchus. He marries off the

---

[67] See Schultz, I, 363–367, for an account of feudal entertainments.

wretched fellow to an old lantern-carrying hag and makes him
a crier of green sauce (ii, 31).

The consultations which play so important a rôle in the
Lancelot play an even more important one in Rabelais.   It
scarcely involves an exaggeration to assert that the whole of
Book iii was inspired by the consultations held for the explanation of dreams, which are so numerous in the *Lancelot*.   The
two essential elements of such an episode are, first, the dream,
and second, the summoning of clerks to interpret it.   We find
the same elements in Rabelais: Panurge's dream and the wise
men called together to explain it—one a theologian, one a physician, one a judge, and the fourth a philosopher.   Rabelais made
no organic change in this essential "donnée."   He merely added
to it without changing its fundamental aspect, and all his addi-
tions are analogous: they consist in Panurge's consulting additional persons, and, receiving no satisfactory answer, in his deter-
mination to journey to the oracle of the Holy Bottle for an
explanation.

The knightly qualities of his heroes are nowhere specifically
set forth in Rabelais.   The reader need not be Aristarchus-eyed,
however, to discover them.   The courtesy and amiability of the
three giants stand out on almost every page; indeed, Pantagruel
is called "le meilleur petit et grand bon hommet que oncques
ceignit espee" (iii, 2) . . . . The valor of Gargantua, Pantagruel,
and Frère Jean shines in contrast with the cowardice of Picrochole, Anarchus, and Panurge . . . . Finally, we have many examples of the liberality of the Rabelaisian hero (i, 45, 46, etc.) ;
and we are told that a noble and generous prince "hath never a
penny, and to hoard up treasure is but a clownish trick" (i, 33).

(b₁) Investitures—

In the *Pantagruel*, upon Maître Alcofribas' reappearance
from his six months' exploration of Pantagruel's interior, the
latter announces to him the conquest, in the interim, of the Land
of the Dipsodes, and invests him with the lordship of Salmigon-

din (II, 32). Grandgousier, in the *Gargantua,* rewards in a most princely manner the members of his household who had assisted in the repulse of Picrochole's hordes. "To Ponocrates he gave Roche-Clermaud; to Gymnast, Coudray; to Eudemon, Montpensier; Rivau, to Tolmère; to Ithybolle, Montsoreau; to Acamas, Cande; Varnes, to Chironacte; Gravot, to Sebast; Quinquenais, to Alexander; Legré, to Sophrone; and so of his other places" (I, 51).

(c₁) *Foundations—*

Frère Jean was still left to be provided for. Grandgousier offered him the abbotcy of Seuillé, but he refused it. Next the king offered him the abbey of Bourgueil, or of Saint Florent, but he was unwilling to assume the charge or government of monks, and asked Grandgousier leave to found an abbey after his own mind and fancy. This request found favor with Gargantua, who offered Frère Jean all his country of Thélème. The Abbey of Thélème constitutes a monument to Rabelais' belief in free will and to his faith in the essential nobility of human nature. The motto of the abbey was: FAIS CE QUE VOULDRAS, "because men that are free, well-born, well-bred, and conversant in honest companions, have naturally an instinct and spur which are called honour that prompteth them unto virtuous actions, and withdraws them from vice" (I, 57).

(d₁) *Authentications—*

Rabelais strove to impart to his narrative an air of reality by employing two formulas, one a literary convention found throughout medieval French literature, the other a trick of the popular romances of his time; the first consists in giving a bookish source for his narrative and connecting it with existent localities, the second in making meticulous use of precise and exact testimony. In *Gargantua* 1 Rabelais pretends that he found an account of the "genealogy and antiquity of Gargantua" in a booklet discovered in an underground tomb of bronze,[68] and by implication he tells his readers that he became acquainted with Pantagruel and his deeds in a "story" (ii, 4, 28) . . . . The peregrinations of Gargantua and Pantagruel leave their traces here and there in a place name or a local curiosity. How did the province of Beauce acquire its name? From the fact that after his mare had felled the forests of the region with her tail, Gargantua observed: "Je trouve *beau ce*" (i, 16). In the succeeding chapter we learn when and under what circumstances Paris was so named. In *Pantagruel* 4 we are told that the great bell of Bourges was nothing else than the gruel bowl of the young Pantagruel.[69] Several additional examples of such authentications occur in the same chapter.

One of the popular elements in Rabelais is the use of statistics, and exact figures which are never round. The appareling of Gargantua, in i, 8, furnishes an example of the first, while the colony of Utopians which Pantagruel transplants into the Land of the Dipsodes (iii, 1) is one of the many illustrations of the latter.

(e₁) Political organization—

Like Britain in the Arthurian Romances, France in the romance of Rabelais is divided into a large number of separate kingdoms, some independent, like Picrochole's, and some tributary. In *Gargantua* 31, the Poitevins, Bretons, Manceaux are referred to as "nations barbares" which are not even the allies of Grandgousier; in chapter 37 Ponocrates wishes he were "roy de Paris" so that he might burn to the ground the infamous Montagu College; in chapter 47 the confederates of Grandgousier who proffer their assistance in repelling Picrochole's onslaught constitute a formidable list; and finally, in *Pantagruel* 4, Gargantua is represented as giving a banquet in honor of "all the princes of his court."

---

[68] Such an artifice is frequent in the romances, but Rabelais' is an imitation of Folengo's in the preface of his *Baldus* (see Thuasne, *Etudes sur Rabelais*, 180–181).

[69] *R. S. S.* IV, 162.

As in the romances, these kingdoms are frequently at war with one another, or with foreign countries. In *Gargantua* 50 three such conflicts are enumerated: the war between Grandgousier and the Bretons, the assault of the barbarians of Spagnola against Grandgousier's ports of Olone and Thalmondois, and the invasion by the Canarians of the province of Onys and the Armorican Islands. Finally, we must not omit to recall the Picrocholine and Dipsodic wars.

(f₁) Position of Grandgousier and Gargantua in the Romance—

Rabelais was careful, in his desire to make his romance conform as closely as it might with his models, to imitate one of their most important, if least obtrusive, characteristics. The aloofness of Arthur in the romances is exaggerated in the aloofness of Grandgousier in the *Gargantua,* and of Gargantua in the *Pantagruel* and the last three books. In *Gargantua* 28, upon receiving the news of Picrochole's onslaught, Grandgousier laments the necessity to which he is put in his old age to don armor and arm himself with lance and mace, but nevertheless the good king quietly stays at home while his son, with his companions, deals with Picrochole. In the *Pantagruel*, Gargantua is never found in the main current of the action after it really gets under way; and more striking still is his detachment from the interests and pursuits of his household in the third book. The reader will recall the pretty touch in III, 35, when Trouillogan, the philosopher, is treating of the "difficulty of marriage" in hair-splitting equivocations: "En cestuy instant Pantagruel aperceut vers la porte de la salle le petit chien de Gargantua, lequel il nommoit Kyne, pource que tel fut le nom du chien de Tobie. Adonc dist à toute la compagnie: 'Nostre roy n'est pas loing d'icy, levons nous.'" A new Pantagruel we have here! Now for the first time Gargantua hears of Panurge's dilemma; yet whatever interest he feels in it, or curiosity in the deliberations of the wise men, is soon dashed by Trouillogan's Pyrrhonism, and he leaves the consultation to proceed without

him . . . . Gargantua does not set out with the others in quest of
the Holy Bottle, naturally, but he sees them off at the port of
embarcation, and in the fourth chapter of the fourth book he
comes into the story for the last time; he sends his squire, Mali-
corne, in the swift Chelidoine with a message for Pantagruel,
who overtakes him at Medamothi on the third day of the voyage—an incident in a way recalling to mind the quest after
a quester in the romances.

§ 4.   WAR IN RABELAIS

There are adventures in the work of Rabelais, and there is no
lack of errantry, but save in one respect the exploits of the Rabelaisian heroes are entirely dissimilar from the usual exploits of
the heroes of the old romances.   Nor do the adventures of the
knight of La Mancha, for that matter, in any wise resemble
those of the Amadises and the Primaleons.   In both Rabelais
and Cervantes the burlesque and the rationalizing intent set
up a peremptory bar against a treatment in the traditional
manner.   The exception, however, in Rabelais is furnished by
the exploits of Gargantua, Pantagruel, and Frère Jean, in the
Picrocholine and Dipsodic wars.

The movement of the Picrocholine War, for example, is precisely that of the wars of the Arthurian Romances.   There is
the summoning of his vassals by a king and his irruption into a
neighbor's territory (I, 26); the messenger announcing the news
to the latter (I, 28); the latter's taking the field with his forces
(I, 48); and finally the battle and the assault of a castle (I, 48).

As in the romances, the exploits of the Rabelaisian heroes
are projected against these wars as a background—the defense
of Seuillé by Frère Jean (I, 27); the rout of a band of pillagers
from Picrochole's army by Gymnaste (I, 34–35); the demoli-
tion of the castle of Vède by Gargantua, Frère Jean, Ponocrates,
Gymnaste, and Eudemon (I, 36, 42–44); and finally the deeds
of valor of Gargantua and Frère Jean at the assault of Roche-
Clermaud (I, 48).

Rabelais greatly diversified and enriched all this medieval matter by profuse borrowings from a great number of various sources but chiefly from contemporary and classical authors. For example, from Geoffroy Tory he drew the episode of the Limousin scholar (II, 6); from Folengo he obtained several of his characters, chief among them Panurge; Francesco Colonna's *Hypnerotomachia Poliphyli,* possibly in conjunction with other Italian sources, such as the *Orlando furioso* (Alcina's palace in canto VII) and Castiglione's *Il Cortegiano* made many contributions of details to the Abbey of Thélème, if they did not actually suggest the main idea; Erasmus furnished many of the views which Rabelais sets forth on war.

To the classics Rabelais is indebted for a good half of his work, according to Plattard.[70] To the ancients he owes a vast number of maxims, allusions, quotations, anecdotes, and illustrative matter. They furnished him, more obviously, numerous citations for many of his parades of recondite learning, as well as incidents in his story. The prologue of the *Gargantua,* for instance, is almost a solid mass of classical lore; for the eleven-month period of gestation which Gargantua underwent he cites eight antique writers (I, 3); for his strange birth he cites several more (I, 6). In support of his statements on the symbolism of white, he marshals eleven classical names. The description of Hell which Epistemon gives in *Pantagruel* 30, and the altered condition there of the mighty and the humble of earth, who have changed estate, is traceable to Lucian's *Menippus seu Necyomantia,* and the exploration of Pantagruel's interior by Maître Alcofribas is closely copied after a similar episode in the *True History* .... These citations might be multiplied indefinitely, but the writer's aim is merely to give a bare idea of Rabelais' literary method.

The formal correspondences, as they have above been set forth, between Rabelais' first two books and the Arthurian Romances

---

[70] See the chapter, ''L'humanisme,'' pp. 171 *seq.,* in his *L'oeuvre de Rabelais,* for a classified list of Rabelais' classical sources.

are clear-cut and specific—especially in the *Gargantua*, where Rabelais' increased mastery of form is strikingly evident—and betray a solicitude which he is at pains to conceal.[71] In the next chapter we shall examine into the nature and contents of the last two books, and shall find in them similarities to the Grail-quest romances which, for all that they are not very obvious and have never before been pointed out, none the less are real, and establish beyond doubt the parentage of this cycle of romances.

---

[71] See Prologue of the *Gargantua*: ''Car à la composition de ce livre seigneurial je ne perdis ne emploiay oncques plus ny aultre temps que celuy qui estoit estably à prendre ma refection corporelle, sçavoir est beuvant et mangeant.''

CHAPTER V

THE QUEST IDEA AS SHOWN IN THE VOYAGE TO THE DIVE BOUTEILLE

I

PRELIMINARY REMARKS

Even in the earliest epics and romances extensive wanderings on the part of the hero were considered essential in order to impart to the narrative an air of exotism and dignity, or in order to introduce into the story the elements of mystery and magic. These elements appear more probable to the reader when a distance in time or space intervenes, when they have the fewest points of contact with everyday reality. In these conditions they excite wonder and pleasure in him.

The ocean has ever been the highway of marvelous travelers. It is on the ocean that Homer launches Ulysses, and Vergil, Aeneas. It is on the ocean that Lucian places the starting point of the marvelous journey in his *True History*. The ocean is the stage of an endless number of medieval journeys.

Journeys on the mysterious and boundless waters form the matter of Irish story tellers especially. Their tales constitute a definite type of story called *imrama,* or "oversea voyages," whose development reached its apex in the eleventh century.[1] The most famous of them is the *Navigatio Sancti Brendani,* a species of Christian Odyssey which in the Middle Ages enjoyed an immense popularity. Written originally in Latin, it was translated or recast, both in verse and prose, into many of the European languages, and profoundly affected their literature.

---

[1] See Meyer and Nutt, *The Voyage of Bran,* I, chaps. 4, 9, and Arthur C. L. Brown, *Mod. Phil.,* XIV, 65–84, "From Cauldron of Plenty to Grail." For a discussion of *Imrama,* see A. C. L. Brown, "Iwain," *Harvard Studies in Philology,* VIII (1903), 56–94.

The story of Saint Brendan has left obvious traces on the body of Grail literature. Dorothy Kempe, in her Introduction to Lonelich's translation of the *Grand Saint Graal*,[2] points out the Brendian elements in this romance. Still clearer are the traces of the legend in parts of the *Perlesvaus* and the *Lancelot du Lac*. These will be considered later.

The seven years' journey of Saint Brendan in search of the Earthly Paradise has two parallels in the Middle Ages, one in reality, the other in fiction, both motivated by powerful spiritual influences of a closely allied nature. The first is the conquest of the Holy Land, the second, the conquest of the Holy Grail.

---

[2] *Early English Text Society, Extra Series*, XCV .... The Judas episode of the *Navigatio*—in which St. Brendan holds converse with Judas, who is imprisoned on a rock in a stormy sea—is faithfully reproduced in *Huon de Bordeaux* (1513); (cf. Lord Berners' translation in *Early English Text Society*, XL, chap. 108).

II

THE HOLY GRAIL IN THE ROMANCES AND IN RABELAIS

In the last eighty years a great discussion has centered about the origin and meaning of the Grail legend. Three chief theories have been proposed to account for it: (1) the conception of the Grail originated in Christian legend connected with the crucifixion of Christ; (2) the legend, originally a Celtic conception, "by a process of glorification and ecclesiasticisation" (Brown), was imperfectly Christianized by the French poets; (3) it sprang from some ritual of the Vegetation Spirit, which survived the fall of the ancient world of paganism and continued down into the Middle Ages.[3] Chrétien de Troyes presumably was the first to introduce the Grail *motif* in the literature of Western Europe, though he only faintly adumbrated the nature and subsequent development of the Grail legend. His successors seized upon the Grail story as they found it in Chrétien, and quickly gave it an extension that, while it preserved and even developed some of its primitive aspects, primarily invested it with a spiritual significance. Also they did not always clearly perceive the meaning and implications of the vessel, either in its original form, or in its new stage of development, and consequently the legend in its evolution and

---

[3] On the Christian theory, see A. Birch-Hirschfeld, *Die Sage vom Gral* (1877), chap. 6; on the Celtic theory, Alfred Nutt, *Studies on the Legend of the Holy Grail* (1888), chap. 7, and A. C. L. Brown, *Mod. Phil.*, XIV, 65–84, and his important articles entitled *The Grail and the English Sir Perceval, Mod. Phil.*, XVI, 553–568, XVII, 361–382, XVIII, 201–228, 661–673, XXII, 79–96; on the Ritual theory, Wm. A. Nitze, *The Fisher King in the Grail Romances, P M L A*, XXIV, 365–418, and Jessie L. Weston, *Legend of Sir Perçeval* (1909) II, *The Quest of the Holy Grail* (1913), *From Ritual to Romance* (1920). For the latest review of the three theories, see J. D. Bruce, *The Evolution of Arthurian Romance* (1923), I, part ii, chaps. 1, 2, 3. Nitze's review of Bruce's work might be read, *Mod. Phil.*, XXII, 99–106. In vol. I, part ii, chap. 8, Bruce briefly reviews the minor theories on the Grail legend.

diffusion went through a number of phases not only not in
accord but often contradictory with one another. Eventually
the legend passed into profane literature with Rabelais, who,
in his burlesque conception of it, exhibits it to us within the
limits of his romance in almost as great a variety of aspects
as he might have found it in the Grail romances printed in his
time.

In the following pages are presented the accidents and properties of the Grail as it appears in Rabelais' parody in Books iv,
and v, and the parallelisms with it found in the romances accessible to him.

Rabelais mentions the Grail four times—once in a letter to
Antoine Hullet, dated the first of March, which Lefranc assigns
to the year 1542,[4] twice in Book iv, and once in Book v.[5]   Here
are the texts:

From the letter to Hullet (Moland, p. 621):

Or vous le ferez, non quand il vous playra, mais quand le vouloir vous
apportera de celluy grand, bon, piteux Dieu, lequel ne créa onques le
quaresme, ouy bien les sallades, arans, merluz, carpes, bechetz, dares,
umbrines, ablettes, rippes, etc. *Item*, les bons vins, singulairement celuy
de veteri enucleando lequel on garde icy a vostre venue, comme ung sang
greal et une seconde, voire quinte essence.

iv, 42: Pantagruel demandoit à quel propous et quelle indication
curative il avoit tant de moustarde en terre projetée. La Royne respondit
que moustarde estoit leur Sangreal et baume céleste: duquel mettant
quelque peu dedans les playes des andouilles terrassées, en bien peu de
temps les navrées guérissoient, les mortes ressuscitoient.

iv, 43: Car on lui avoit robbé une veze pleine de vent propre que jadis
à Ulysses donna le bon ronfleur Aeolus pour guider sa nauf en temps calme.
Lequel il gardoit religieusement comme ung autre Sangreal, et en gueris-
soit plusieurs enormes maladies....

---

[4] Lefranc, Chronology, I.

[5] It is noteworthy that each one of these allusions occurs during the
second part of Rabelais' productive period, the first probably about the
time he was projecting the last three books. Though this point should not
too strongly be insisted upon, nevertheless it would seem that if the Grail
is mentioned only synchronously with the second part of his work, and
mentioned relatively so frequently, there must have been a close connection in his mind between the two.

v, 10: Là aussi nous dist estre un flasque de Sang greal[6] chose divine et à peu de gens conneue.

Finally, in v, 44, the Holy Bottle is introduced, which, though not specifically so called, is *the* Grail in Rabelais. Herewith is its description: ". . . . la sacrée Bouteille, toute revestue de pur et beau cristalin en forme ovale, excepté que le limbe estoit quelque peu patent plus qu'icelle forme ne porteroit." In v, 45, in answer to Panurge's question, the Bottle utters the mystic word, *Trinc!*

It is clear that Rabelais in his parody varied from time to time his burlesque conception of the Grail. In the passages quoted above the Grail either is described as possessing, or is joined with similarly endowed objects possessing, the following forms:

A. FORMS[7]

(*a*) In v, 10, it is a liquid—the Holy Blood. In addition, in the letter to Hullet it is introduced in connection with the word "vins."

(*b*) In iv, 42, mustard with curative powers is likened to it.

(*c*) In iv, 43, wind likewise endowed is linked with it.

(*d*) In v, 44, it is by implication a bottle.

---

[6] Rabelais has the spellings *Sang greal* and *Sangreal* twice each. In v, 10, he very obviously confuses the Grail with the *Holy Blood.* He could have taken this trait either from the *Perlesvaus* or the *Grand Saint Graal.* The forms *Sang greal* and *Sangreal*, however, are not found in the romances just mentioned. They are burlesque forms of his own or the repetition of forms current at the time he was writing. Bruce, *Evolution of Arthurian Romance* (1923), I, 255, note 37, says: " 'Saint Greal,' in the later romances (fifteenth century), owing to a false division of the two words, came to be understood as 'Sang Real'—i.e., Blood Royal, meaning the Blood of Christ, which the Grail was supposed to contain." W. Hertz, *Parzival von Wolfram von Eschenbach, neu bearbeitet* (1898), says at p. 424: "To it [the dish in which Joseph collected the Blood of Christ], as the most important hallow, was also added the false interpretation, current in the later Middle Ages, of the word *San-Greal*, Holy Dish, as *Sangreal*, royal blood. This interpretation Oswald von Wolkenstein seems to have in mind when he says that Christ redeemed the fall of Adam with his *grâl.* Also Rabelais in his parody uses the expression in this sense when he relates how, in the Isle de Cassade, *ung flasque de Sangreal* was shown with the greatest solemnity." Consult the *New English Dictionary* under *Sangrail, Sang royal, Sanke royal*, and Godefroy, *Complement*, under *Sanc.* On blood relics in the Middle Ages, see Hertz, 454–455.

[7] Wm. A. Nitze, *P M L A*, XXIV, 406: "Hence it becomes technically possible as in P [*Peredur*] to have a Grail romance in which the Grail is replaced by an equivalent; namely the head on a salver." In the *Parzival* it is a stone, the *lapis exilis.*

B. VIRTUES

Of the four times that Rabelais mentions the Grail, only twice does he attribute to it magical qualities. In the letter to Hullet it is merely associated with wine. In v, 10, it is apparently identified with the relics of Glastonbury, of which Rabelais, as a monk, might know (cf. note 8, p. 213). In neither of these two cases is anything more than a certain curiosity, or at the most oddity—especially in the second—implied about it. However, in the passages from Book ɪᴠ, the idea of magical healing is specifically set forth in association with it. We are told in ɪᴠ, 42, that mustard has the virtue of healing the wounded, and resuscitating the dead; and in ɪᴠ, 43, that wind has the virtue of overcoming the gravest maladies. Finally, the Holy Bottle shares with the Grail its ability to counsel and prophesy.

Stated briefly, Rabelais associates the Grail with objects endowed with the following attributes:

(*a*) With the power of physical refection (letter to Hullet).

(*b*) With the power of healing (ɪᴠ, 42, 43).

(*c*) With the power to counsel and prophesy (the Holy Bottle).

C. MISCELLANEOUS ATTRIBUTES

These additional traits should be noted:

First, the Grail is located on various so to say inaccessible islands of the mysterious ocean, and in Cathay.

Second, on two occasions when the Grail appears before the entire company, or Panurge alone, an elaborate ceremonial is prescribed. ''Panurge fit tant par belles prieres avec les syndics du lieu qu'ils le nous monstrèrent; mais ce fut avec plus de cérémonies et solennité plus grande trois fois qu'on ne monstre à Florence les Pandectes de Justinian, ne la Veronique à Rome'' (v, 10). The ceremonial of the Holy Bottle, in v, 44–45, is too long and elaborate to be given in its entirety. Suffice it to say that Panurge was clad in a green gaberdine (the Grail is associated in the *Grand Saint Graal* with a *green* corporale,

Hertz, p. 504) in order to appear before the shrine of the Bottle, that he went through a complicated ritual before the Bottle was sufficiently propitiated to utter the prophetic word.

Third, it is usually provided with a large body of guards and keepers (cf. v, 35).

Turning to the list and the table of romances in the second chapter, the reader will see that there were in print and easily accessible to Rabelais when he wrote the last three books the following romances dealing with the Holy Grail and its history:

L'hystoire du Saint Graal (see p. 156 for the contents of this romance).

Lancelot du Lac (part 4, *La Queste du Saint Graal*).

Perceval le Gallois (preceded by *L'Elucidation du Saint Graal*).

Merlin.

Of these four romances, Rabelais mentions only the *Lancelot* and the *Merlin.* However, in the four passages where he directly alludes to the Grail, and in the attributes which he assigns to the Holy Bottle, he invests his Grail with such a large and varied number of 'traits' as to lead one to the conclusion that his acquaintance with the Grail romances extant in his day went beyond these two romances.

From these four romances what information might Rabelais have gathered concerning the characteristics and attributes of the Grail? For ease of reference, the 'traits' attributed to the Grail in the romances and in Rabelais have been classified similarly.

A₁. FORMS

(*a*) The Grail is the Dish —"ung plat ou escuelle"— of the Last Supper, in which Joseph of Arimathea collected the blood from the wounds of Christ on the cross. (*L'hystoire du Saint Graal*, 1516, ff. 5–6.)

(*b*) It is a chalice-shaped vessel of great beauty and bright-ness, of some unknown material, and suggesting a lamp. (*Lancelot*, 1533, second part, f. 51; third part, f. 59.)

(*c*) It is not clear what the Grail is meant to be. (*Perceval*.)[8]

---

[8] See 1918 reprint of *Perceval* (1530), Payot and Co., Paris.

It is not clear what Chrétien meant the Grail to be. (On the word *Graal* in the romances, see Birch-Hirschfeld, 187–188; for the latest views on the word, see Wm. A. Nitze, *Mod. Phil.*, XIII, 185 *seq.*, and Bruce, I, 253–255). Chrétien always calls it *graal* and never *Saint Graal*, though he does say that it is *saintisme*. He has only one passage that ascribes sanctity to the vessel, in that the Grail is such a holy thing that the father of the Fisher King is sufficiently nourished by a single *oiste* brought to him in it (7796–7799). In the *Chronicle of Helinandus* (Paulin Paris, *Les Romans de la Table Ronde*, I, 90) the vessel is described as a "scutella lata et aliquantulum profunda, in qua pretiosae dapes, cum suo jure, solent apponi et dicitur nomine Graal." In the same entry (for the year 717) it is con-nected with the Dish of the Last Supper ".... de catino illo vel paropsodie in quo dominus coenavit cum discipulis suis." When the Crusaders cap-tured Caesarea in 1101 "a flat, saucer-like, hexagonal dish of emerald-colored glass" fell to the Genoese in their portion of the spoils. Later a tradition arose that this vessel had been used at the Last Supper, its sub-stance having become miraculously changed into emerald (Bruce, I, 360–362). Several other traditions of the Grail were current in the Middle Ages: the large silver cup called *Calix domini*, containing a sponge said to have been the one used on the lips of Christ; two vessels containing blood from Christ's wounds, brought, according to tradition, by Joseph of Arimathea to Glastonbury and there buried with his body, in com-memoration whereof the escutcheon of Glastonbury was a cross with drops and two phials (John Colin Dunlop, *History of Fiction*, revised with notes and appendix by Henry Wilson (1906), I, 463–470; Birch-Hirschfeld, p. 223 and note 2; W. Hertz, *Parzival von Wolfram von Eschenbach, neu bear-beitet* (1898), 456–458.) In *Le Grand Saint Graal* the Grail is the cup of the Last Supper: "lescuele en lequele le fiex dieu avoit mangiet" (Som-mer, I, 13). Joseph celebrates the first Eucharistic sacrament ("le sacre-ment de ma chair & de mon sanc") in a chalice. In the chalice are *pain* and *vins* called *saint boire* (Sommer, I, 40). In *Lestoire de Merlin* this chalice came from heaven. Robert de Boron makes Christ thus speak of it in his discourse to Joseph:

> Cest vaisseau ou mien sanc meis
> Quant de mon cors le requeillis
> Calices apelez sera....

But Robert identifies the Grail with the dish of the last supper also 395 *seq.*, 433 *seq.*, 507 *seq.*, 563 *seq.* Cf. Bruce, I, 245.

In the Vulgate *Merlin* and *Perlesvaus* the Grail is the vessel in which Joseph of Arimathea received the blood from the wound of Christ on the cross (Nutt, *The Legend of the Holy Grail* (1888), p. 69). In Wolfram's *Parzival* the Grail is a stone, the *lapis exilis*. It has no direct connection with the Passion of Christ (Nutt, p. 66) save that its virtues are renewed every Holy Friday by a dove from heaven, which places a host on the Grail. So with Wolfram the Grail is a reflection of those precious stones which medieval superstition endowed with curative powers.

B₁. VIRTUES

(*a*) The Grail has the power of physical refection. (In the
Perceval, 1530, f. 218, the Grail appears daily and serves to
Arthur and his court the delicacies each could desire.[9]   It has
the same virtue in *Lancelot,* 1533, second part, ff. 51, 85; third
part, f. 68; in *L'hystoire du Saint Graal,* 1516, ff. 91, 104, etc.[10])

---

[9] Cf. Rabelais, v, 43: "Icy de mesmes beuvans de ceste liqueur mirifique
sentirez goust de tel vin comme l'aurez imaginé.   Or imaginez et beuvez."

[10] In Chrétien the word *graal* is a common noun and designates simply
a dish of some sort used in conveying food to an unseen person.   With his
successors the word was made a proper noun, was regularly preceded by the
adjective *saint,* and the vessel became a mystical talisman endowed with
supernatural powers of various kinds.
  Its chief function in the old romances, except in Chrétien and Robert,
is to supply with food and often wine.   .This idea is first distinctly met
with in Pseudo-Wauchier, 20114 *seq.,* where the Grail performs the
service at a supper and supplies the tables with meat and drink (see Bruce,
I, 294, note 10, for magical objects in folklore with food-producing powers,
and a distinction between these and the miracle of the multiplied fish in
Robert).   In *Le Grand Saint Graal* (Sommer, I, 216) it multiplies twelve
loaves of bread into five hundred, and a fish cut in four into such a large
number of pieces that the whole is sufficient to feed Joseph and his five
hundred companions.   In the *Lancelot du Lac* (Sommer, V, 393) it daily
feeds Pelles and his household.   In the *Parzival* it has the same qualities of
refection.   In *Le Grand Saint Graal* (Sommer, I, 250) it furnishes with all
the good viands the heart of each could desire.   The food provided by the
Grail, accordingly, is adapted to the tastes of all: each knight has such
meats and drinks as he loves best in the world.
  The refection furnished by the Grail is also spiritual, but for the elect
only: "Et maintenant tous ceux auxquels il sera donné de voir d'un coeur
pur le vase que je te confie seront des miens: ils auront satisfaction de
coeur, et joie perdurable" (Paulin Paris, I, 132, 142, 277; Bruce, I, 237–
238: "With Robert .... it is a vessel of 'grace' in whose service only the
good and pure can remain").
  Another function of the Grail is to counsel and prophesy.   So in *Le
Saint Graal* Joseph of Arimathea, by kneeling and praying before the
Grail, obtains counsel and aid from the Holy Ghost (Paulin Paris, I, 145,
148, 197).   Likewise in the *Parzival* (Weston's translation, IX, 865–866)
the Grail promises aid to the Grail knights praying before it in order to
beseech a cure for King Amfortas.
  Among the more remarkable powers of the Grail is its ability to heal.
Two noteworthy examples occur in the *Lancelot.*   When Lancelot was con-
ducted, for the second time, under a spell, to the bed of Helayne, the
mother of Galahad, he was discovered by Guenevere, who in her anger
bade him go away forever.   In his grief he was visited with one of his
fits of madness, and wandered long through the country as a wild man.   In
the fourth year of his affliction he chanced to come to Corbenic, where
months afterwards, he was recognized by Helayne.   King Pelles had him
bound and put in a bed.   In the night the Grail goes about in the palace,

(*b*) It has the power of healing (*Lancelot,* 1533, third part, ff. 59, 62, 76, etc.).

(*c*) It has the ability to counsel and prophesy. (In the *Grand Saint Graal* it exercises this power directly; in *L'hystoire du Saint Graal,* 1516, its power to counsel and prophesy seems to be exercised on a few occasions through an associated supernatural voice (f. 101), or through a supernatural monitor (f. 118); but in general it is exercised through the keepers of the Grail—Joseph and his son Josephe (ff. 103, 107, etc.).[11]

C₁. MISCELLANEOUS ATTRIBUTES

First, the Grail resides in places accessible in some romances to ordinary mortals, and inaccessible in others.[12] (In *L'hystoire*

---

and as soon as Lancelot sets eyes on it he is healed (Sommer V, 398–400; *Lancelot* (1533), third part, f. 62). The second example is the cure it operates on Perceval and a strange knight who turns out to be Hector des Mares. The two meet and, not recognizing each other, battle long and desperately, until they fall to the ground mortally wounded. As they feel death approaching a great brightness suddenly surrounds them. They see a chalice-shaped vessel draw near them, preceded and followed by two lighted tapers. Instinctively they reverently bow their heads before the vessel, and immediately they are healed and the vessel vanishes (Sommer, V, 392; *Lancelot* (1533), third part, f. 59).

[11] In *L'hystoire du Saint Graal* (1516), ff. 227–228 (228–229, correctly), is reproduced the story from the *Lancelot* (see *infra* p. 222 and note 21) of the adventures of Lancelot and Galahad during their six-months' journey together on the ship in quest of the Grail. In each romance Lancelot is started on this adventure in the same way: he is asleep in the midst of a forest and waters when he hears a voice which bids him rise, arm himself, and enter into the first ship he should encounter. Upon opening his eyes he finds himself enveloped in a *grant clerté*. But the conclusions of the versions show an interesting variant. In the *Lancelot* we read: "En icelle nef demourerent Lancelot et Galahad bien demy an et plus ... et par plusieurs foys arriverent en ysles estranges ou il ne repairoit sinon bestes sauvages et y trouverent aventures merveilleuses lesquelles ils misrent a fin tant par leur proesse que *par la grace du saint esperit* qui en tous lieux leur aydoit" (f. 111). *L'hystoire du Saint Graal* has this reading: " .... lesquelles ils misrent a fin tant par leur proesse que *par la grace du sainct greal* qui en tous lieux leur aydoit." The variant in *L'hystoire* very likely identifies the voice and the *grant clerté* with the Grail, thus bringing the vessel in line with its power to counsel and prophesy, adverted to in the first part of the romance.

[12] The location of the Grail in the old romances is, so to say, in a state of flux. In some of the romances it possesses a single habitation, which it does not leave, as in the *Parzival;* in others, as in the *Queste,* it travels about—it is here today, gone tomorrow. Again, in several romances, the

du Saint Graal, 1516, f. 119, the Grail is said to have been visited by many knights; see also the citations from the *Lancelot* under B₁ above).

Second, when the Grail appears before the quester, it is usually seen in a pageant (*Perceval, L'hystoire du Saint Graal,* 1516, f. 145).[13]

Third, the Grail in the romances always has a keeper, usually a king, who is attended by a retinue (*Perceforest,* 1531, part vi, f. 116, and citations from the *Lancelot*).[14]

Grail is located in an inaccessible place, as in the *Perceval* and the German cycle; in others it is no wise so, as in the *Lancelot,* where Gawain, Lancelot, and Bohors visit the Grail castle more than once (Sommer, IV, 339; V, 105; V, 139, 294). In general, Corbenic is, in the French romances, the permanent home of the Grail. Frequently the vessel is visible to all but the impure and the unchaste. So in the *Perlesvaus* it fails to appear before Lancelot because of his guilty love for Guenevere.

In the Perceval romances, the Grail resides in the castle of the Fisher King. In the *Parzival* it is kept at Montsalvatch (Mons salvationis), which is located in the Pyrenees, near Barcelona. In *Der jüngere Titurel* the Grail legend is married to that of Prester John (Hertz, pp. 453, 549). In it the Grail and its guardians, Parzival, Lohengrin, Kondwiramur, and the Templars, in the train of Arthur and all his chivalry, carry the Grail to India, into the realms of Prester John, and it dwells to this day with its guardians in the remote places of the Eastern world. In the *Queste* the Grail is finally assumed to heaven itself.

On this, see Wm. A. Nitze, *P M L A,* XXIV, at p. 375.

[13] The first time we meet the Grail in the old romances—in the *Perceval*—it appears in a pageant. As the pageant lends itself very readily to decoration, in the subsequent romances it was extended and became highly developed. One of the most decorative of these pageants occurs in *Le Saint Graal.*

In Chrétien, Perceval sees in the palace of the Fisher King a youth coming from a room, bearing a lance whose point drops blood. He is followed by two youths, who pass through the hall where Perceval is, and who go to another room. They carry ten-branched candlesticks all aflame with candles. These are followed by a maiden, who in both her hands carries a dish (the Grail). She is followed by another maiden carrying a small silver platter (3152–3204). In one of Gawain's visits to Corbenic the Grail is carried around the tables by maidens and fills the plates of all, save Gawain. In *Le Saint Graal* (Dunlop (1906), I, 478) eight angels carry the Grail and other hallows in procession before Joseph. In brief, in the romances in general, the Grail castle is a place of highest reverence, and all things concerning the Grail are done with ceremonial solemnity and after a prescribed order. It should be noted, however, that in the later accounts, in the *Queste,* for instance, there are no more ceremonials, no more processions, for the Grail has left its home and is going about through the land.

[14] In the old romances there are two different lines of keepers. In Chrétien the keeper is called the Fisher King and his name and lineage

Comparing the conception and treatment of the Grail in Rabelais and in the romances, we notice a remarkable number of parallelisms. The only striking departure Rabelais shows from his models is in the fourfold form he assigns to his Grail,[15] and the broad burlesque that permeates each one of his different conceptions of it. Naturally, nowhere in the romances is the Grail likened to wine, or mustard, or anything like them, or even to a bottle. But the diversity of aspects under which it appears in the various romances was of itself enough to suggest to Rabelais that in this respect at least his burlesque fancy might be allowed absolutely free scope. It must be pointed out, however, that in what is *the* Grail in Rabelais, that is the Bottle, the departure from the form or forms of the traditional vessel has nothing abrupt, or shocking, or unconvincing about it.

---

are not disclosed. In the Grail cycle Joseph of Arimathea is the first guardian of the Grail. It is not made clear who his successor is after he has passed from the scene. Robert de Boron has Brons, his brother-in-law, succeed him; in *Le Grand Saint Graal* his successor is his son Josephe. In some of the romances the generations between Josephe and Perceval are bridged over by a single keeper, Brons, the grandfather of Perceval, who is to remain on earth until Perceval shall have come to the castle and achieved the Quest, when the Fisher King is to remit to him the Grail and the other hallows. In *Le Grand Saint Graal* the keepers dwell in Corbenic, and their succession is tolerably clear. Joshua, Alain's brother, married the daughter of Alphasem, and ten days after both Alain and Alphasem (the keepers) died. After Joshua the warders were his direct descendants in succession: Eminadap, his son; Katheloys, son of Eminadap; from him was born Manaal, from him Lambor. All were called *riche pescheours*. After Lambor, his son Pellehan reigned. Pellehan was succeeded by Pelles, the father of Helayne, the mother of Galahad, who achieved the adventures in which the others had failed. This is the version followed in the *Lancelot*. On the confusion of the two lines of keepers, see Bruce I, 392.

[15] Notes 6, 7, and 8 have made it amply clear that the authors of the old romances did not consider themselves obligated to follow Chrétien and Robert and adopt slavishly their conception of what the Grail was.

III

WHAT THE QUEST OF THE HOLY GRAIL IS

In the old romances, especially in *La Queste du Saint Graal* (the Galahad quest), the quest of the Grail is a quest after knightly, and, above all, after Christian perfection. The aim of the knight is to pattern his own life after the example of Christ. In the *Perlesvaus* the true ideal of chivalry is

. . . .not the practice of courtly love, or the quest of mere adventure, but the service of Christianity. The knight that craves glory shall fight for his faith and convert the heathen. Thus the quest of the Grail will be the successful accomplishment of a war waged for the good of the church, and the holy vessel itself will stand for the spiritual goal which many will seek but only the perfect will attain.[16]

In its initiation, the quest was a quest militant whose chief aim was the subversion of paganism. In its development, however, the ideal became modified. The enemy no longer was the pagan invader, but the pagan within man's heart: his passions, his desires, his appetites. The successful quester was he who, in sackcloth—literally, as with Lancelot, or figuratively, as with Galahad—succeeded best in mortifying the flesh. Yet this was not the end of the quest—it was merely a necessary condition to success. The quest of the Holy Grail, in the end, became a quest after mystic communion with God,[17] attainable by the blameless knight alone. It was moved by counsels of perfection consisting of the three qualities: (*a*) voluntary poverty, (*b*) entire obedience, (*c*) perfect chastity.

---

[16] See Wm. A. Nitze, *Perlesvaus* (Johns Hopkins dissertation, 1902), p. 45. On the spirit of asceticism and idealism that moved the questers, see Bruce, I, 379, 420, 423, 424, and Hertz, p. 447.

[17] Paulin Paris, I, 142 (*Joseph d'Arimathie* or *Le Saint Graal*, the prose redaction): ''Bientôt ceux qui étaient assis furent pénétrés, d'une douceur ineffable qui leur fit tout oublier.''

No less than the romance quest, the quest in Rabelais is a quest after perfection. But the ideal of perfection has changed. In Rabelais it is not the glowing faith that uplifts man face to face with God; it is faith of another sort, faith in the beneficence of Knowledge, in the beauty of Wisdom, in the power and might of Truth. The quest of Pantagruel is a crusade against Error. "Si Pantagruel parcourt le monde c'est pour regarder face à face toutes les illusions, se mesurer avec les chimères dangereuses, affronter dans leurs repaires les sottises malfaisantes."[18]

This, then, is the meaning of the wine of the Bottle. This wine is a "divine liqueur . . . . qui tient toute verité enclose" (v, 45). It is, accordingly, no ordinary wine, since filled with it the Bottle is filled with mysteries (v, 45); it is a wine which makes man divine, "pouvoir il a d'emplir l'ame de toute verité tout savior et philosophie" (v, 46). In brief it is wine considered in its pagan mystical aspects, such as it was invested with in the worship of Dionysus among the Greeks.[19]

Just as in the romances there are necessary conditions of attainment to the Grail, so with Rabelais. Both the romance quest and Rabelais' exact sacrifices and impose self-abnegation. In the romances, in order to contemplate God, one's clarity of vision must not be troubled by the fleshly appetites, and the quester must give himself up wholesouledly to his quest. It is precisely the same in Rabelais. Knowledge, Wisdom, Truth are jealous mistresses; they likewise demand sincere service and a high intent. In consequence, wine in its purely material aspect, and with all its implications, must be foresworn by the questers, for ". . . . tous personnages qui s'adonnent et dedient à contemplation des choses divines, doivent en tranquillité leurs esprits maintenir, hors toute perturbation des sens: laquelle plus est manifestée en yvrognerie qu'en autre passion, quelle qu'elle soit" (v, 34).

---

[18] Emile Gebhart, *Rabelais, la renaissance et la réforme* (1895), p. 66.
[19] See Walter Pater, *Greek Studies*, pp. 1 *seq.*

IV

THE GRAIL QUEST

In the old romances, the quest of the Holy Grail is a quest by land. But three times at least in his quest the hero ventured on the waters in far-off journeys which lasted many days. In the *Parzival* we learn of the hero

> Nu tuot uns di aventiure bekant
> er habe erstrichen manec lant
> z'ors, unt in schiffen uf dem wac.

IX, 41–43.

In the *Perlesvaus* and in the *Lancelot du Lac* both Perceval and Lancelot sail the seas in their search for the Holy Vessel. These journeys are remarkable enough to require that their substance be given.

In the *Perlesvaus*,[20] as a result of the saintly works of Perceval, the land of Britain was becoming Christianized. A troop of pagans, who obstinately persisted in their denial of the New Law, determined to leave the land, and set out to sea in a ship. But Perceval overtook them on the shore and slew many of them; the rest jumped into the ship, where Perceval followed them and slaughtered them, save the pilot, who forthwith accepted the New Law. Meantime the ship, with sails set, was fast gaining the open sea. Soon it was out of sight of the land and continued to go swiftly, guided by God. It sailed by night and by day, until it reached an island in the sea on which stood a castle. Perceval landed and entered the castle and found it the fairest ever he had seen. He discovered that it was under the guardianship of two hermits who were men before the death of Christ, and had known Joseph of Arimathea before Christ was crucified. In the castle Perceval saw many wonders happen

---

[20] Potvin, *Perceval le Gallois*, I, 323, 327–338. *L'hystoire du Saint Graal* (1516), ff. 206–208, repeats this episode of the *Perlesvaus*.

before his eyes, but the hermits refused to give an explanation
of them. They told him about two neighboring islands, one the
Island of Plenty, the other the Island of Poverty. The kings of
the Island of Plenty who did not by their works win divine
approval were exiled to the Island of Poverty. The hermits
informed Perceval that after his adventures should all be com-
pleted he would return to them and be crowned king of the
Island of Plenty. They harbored him for the night, and next
day he boarded his ship and set forth. Directed by God, the
ship, after days and nights of sailing, reached an island whereon
was an ancient castle which had known better days. Perceval
learned from its mistress that she was the wife of one of his
uncles, and that since his death the land had been ravaged by
the pagan folk. She had two daughters who dwelt with her,
and a son who now was a prisoner of the king of the Island
of the Whale. Perceval promised to free them from their
oppressor and to rescue his cousin. The next morning he set
out to sea and speedily reached the Island of the Whale.
After divers adventures he rescued his cousin, as well as a
maiden who also was a captive on the island. After having
restored his cousin to his mother, Perceval again took to the
high sea. After a time he reached an island whereon he
beheld a burning castle which was tenanted by a solitary
hermit. Perceval learned from the hermit that this was the
castle in which his cousin Joshua slew his own mother, that it
had been burning ever since then and would continue to burn
until the day when it should kindle the fire which was to destroy
the world. Perceval did not tarry there, but hurried away in
great haste. He passed three kingdoms and sailed many waters,
skirting many deserts on one side and another of the sea, until
one day he reached an island on which dwelt twelve hermits who
were the caretakers of twelve tombs. In these lay buried Alain li
gros, Perceval's father, and his eleven brothers. On the following
day Perceval departed and after the ship had sailed swiftly and
far, he reached the island of Great Britain, where he disembarked.

This adventure is not an episode in Perceval's quest after the Grail, as before entering upon it he had achieved the quest. It is, however, an episode in his quest after holiness and sanctity, of which the visible Grail is a symbol and prefigurement. The sea voyage on which Lancelot engaged[21], on the other hand, is one of the adventures that befell him in the course of his search after the sacred vessel.

Lancelot, having undertaken the quest in atonement of his sins, found himself after a time alone and abandoned in a deserted region surrounded by forests and waters. He prayed to God to have pity on him, and in answer a voice bade him go to the sea, where he would find a ship which he should board. This was the Ship of Solomon, and on it Lancelot found the body of Perceval's sister. The ship began to move, and soon after arrived at a small rocky island, on which Lancelot found a hermit. After receiving encouragement from the holy man to persist in the path of holiness, Lancelot again boarded the ship, which bore him away. After sailing for a month, he arrived at a wooded shore. There a knight came to him and joined him. The knight was Galahad, and father and son were glad for each other's company. They remained together on the ship six months and more, and many times touched at strange islands peopled with beasts, and where marvelous adventures befell them. The story does not record them, as it would require too much time. One day the ship again arrived at a wooded shore, where there was a cross. A white knight leading a charger approached them, and greeting them addressed himself to Galahad: "God bids you leave this ship, mount this charger, and achieve the adventures of Logres." Lancelot remained on the ship, which continued its voyaging, until one night it stopped at the foot of a castle. A voice spoke to Lancelot, saying: "Go ashore and enter the castle; there you will see part of what you long to see." Lancelot obeyed. He approached the castle (it was Corbenic), which was guarded by two lions. They did not molest

21 Sommer, VI, 177–182, *Lancelot* (1533), third part, ff. 110–113.

him. In the castle all were asleep, as it was after midnight.
Lancelot wandered from room to room, hoping to find out in
what part of the world he was. At last he came to a door which
he could not open. He listened and heard a voice sweetly sing-
ing: "Glory, praise, and honor to the Father in Heaven."
Lancelot kneeled and devoutly prayed to the Lord to allow him
to behold the Holy Grail. His prayer was heard, the door
opened, and a dazzling brightness emanated from the room.
Joyfully Lancelot approached the door; a voice warned him not
to enter. Through the open door Lancelot saw on a silver table
the Holy Grail covered with red samite, and before it a priest
celebrating mass. As the priest raised the host as though to show
it to the people, it seemed to Lancelot that he was unable to bear
its weight. Disregarding the warning, Lancelot rushed to the
priest's aid, praying to Christ to forgive him his disobedience.
As he entered the room he was struck by a fiery wind; he fell
down as if dead; he felt hands seize him and remove him from
the room. On the morrow the people of the castle found him
sitting at the door, unable to speak or move. Fourteen days he
remained in this condition—one day for each year he had dwelt
in sin. On the fifteenth day he opened his eyes and spoke. He
asked how he had come to the castle. After being fully informed
by those about him he asked for the hair-cloth shirt he had worn
on the quest, but he was told not to trouble about it, as his
quest was ended.

It is at once obvious that in the two marvelous journeys by
sea of Perceval and Lancelot we have before us an imitation of
the *imrama*, or Celtic "oversea voyages," spoken of at the beginning of this chapter. It would require no great boldness to
assert that the specific *imram* which served as their model was
the *Navigatio Sancti Brendani*. In the first place, we have no
good reason to think that any of these peculiarly Irish stories
were known on the continent at the time, besides the *Navigatio;*
in the second, the details of Saint Brendan's voyage agree fairly
well with the details of the voyages of the two Grail questers.

The ships of the questers sail about on the ocean directed only by the Lord's will and with no definite itinerary before them. So does Saint Brendan's. In their voyages, like Saint Brendan, they touch at many islands. In the case of Lancelot, these islands are tenanted by beasts only; the islands Perceval chances upon in his journeyings are tenanted by people alone—usually hermits. In the *Navigatio*, on the other hand, we run across an Island of Birds, an Island of Sheep, and an Island of Sea Snails. On these, besides the animals which are their chief tenants, we find hermits as well. Perceval, we recall, chanced upon an Island of the Whale, which may be the Jasconius of the *Navigatio*, and he is told of an Island of Plenty, which may be the Earthly Paradise, in the quest of which Saint Brendan set out on his seven years' journey. It is a question, apparently, of what phase of the *Navigatio* the authors of the *Perlesvaus* and of the *Lancelot* stressed. In each case, finally, the hero experienced marvelous adventures and returned to his own land, marvelously guided.

Now it can admit of little doubt that Rabelais had read one of the Perceval romances, and certainly the *Lancelot*. There is clear evidence also that he was familiar with the legend of Saint Brendan.[22] It seems possible that having read the passages from the *Perceval* and the *Lancelot* he patterned his quest of the Bottle after the two episodes sketched above, and, using them as a nucleus, expanded them by intussusception—as he so well knew how to do—drawing from the following sources:

(1) The Italian romances, chiefly Folengo's,
(2) The popular romances,
(3) Medieval literature:
    (a) *Saint Brendan's Voyage,*
    (b) The Arthurian Romances,
    (c) Various medieval works,
(4) Classical literature,
(5) Contemporary literature and accounts of travelers,
(6) His own imagination.

---

[22] See Tilley, *François Rabelais,* 252.

From Folengo he obtained the idea of the episode of the sheep (IV, 5–8), and probably of the storm (IV, 18–22), though storms are a commonplace in all the romances. He owes to the *Disciple de Pantagruel* the story of Bringuenarilles (IV, 17), possibly of Wild Island and its Chitterlings (IV, 35–42), and of the Island of Tools (V, 9). He is indebted to *Saint Brendan's Voyage* for the sea monster—the Physetere—which attacks the fleet (IV, 33–34), for the Ringing Island (V, 1–8), for V, 34, which, it seems probable, is copied after the Island of Raisins of the *Navigatio,* and for the Island of Macreons (IV, 26). The romances of the Round Table leave their traces chiefly in Rabelais' conception and treatment of the Grail, in the long consultation of Book III, undertaken to resolve Panurge's doubts, and in the Islands of the Chitterlings and of Lent, which very likely are amplified copies of the Islands of Plenty and of Poverty in the *Perceval.* The influence of other forms of medieval literature is too fugitive to deserve cataloguing here.

From the classics he drew chiefly his idea of Lantern-land (V, 32–33), which obviously is suggested by a similar country in Lucian's *True History,* and tales such as that of the death of Pan (IV, 28). From contemporary literature he copied his apologue of Physie and Antiphysie (IV, 32), which he owes to Cilio Calcagnini; the fantastic story of the Frozen Words (IV, 50–51), which may be found in Castiglione; and the description of the temple of the Bottle, which is literally translated from Francesco Colonna's *Hypnerotomachia Poliphyli.* He made use of the accounts of travelers in various chapters, especially in the Country of Satin (V, 30–31). Finally, to his own invention are probably to be credited the satirical parts of the last two books, such as his travesty on justice and the law courts (V, 11–15), on Lent (IV, 29–32), on religious fanatics (IV, 45–54).[23]

---

[23] This list does not purport to catalogue completely Rabelais' sources. It is designed merely to give a general idea of his mode of composition. For fairly complete catalogues of his sources, except the medieval, which have hitherto been slighted, see W. F. Smith, *Rabelais in his Writings,* Plattard, *L'Oeuvre de Rabelais,* Fleury, *Rabelais et ses oeuvres.*

In fine, the voyage of Books iv and v differs from those of
Saint Brendan and Perceval and Lancelot in that it has a definite itinerary; it agrees with them in that Pantagruel and his
company are launched on the bosom of the mysterious ocean,[24]
in that they meet with and land at a great number of strange
islands, where they, too, have marvelous adventures, and in that
the end of all four of them is the same: to achieve a sovereign
good.

---

[24] Although the duration, route, stops, and the objective of his voyage
are all carefully planned, yet Rabelais manages to envelop the travels of
his company in an air of mystery. For instance, ''Medamothi'' is ''no
land,'' and to emphasize this he makes it an important mart for a non-
existent Afro-Asiatic trade, and situates it at a distance of only two hours'
pigeon flight from France. In the Island of Ennasin, which would be only
four hours of pigeon flight—500 miles at the most—from France, already
the land from which the questers hailed is called ''l'aultre monde,'' showing that Rabelais' ocean is the mysterious, uncharted ocean of legend.

CHAPTER VI

THE MARVELOUS IN RABELAIS

No part of Rabelais' work is more characteristic of his peculiar genius than is his treatment of the marvelous. In it we find a capital illustration of the dissonant elements that have made of him from his day to ours a puzzle to the critic and interpreter. In his use of the marvelous he mingled ancient and medieval natural lore, which, however, he subjected to the modern scientific attitude of skepticism.[1]

Naturally, Rabelais' scientific 'facts' are those of his day. They are a legacy of antiquity still further distorted by their tradition to modern times through the Middle Ages with all their superstition, their credulity, their indisposition to observe and reason, and their inordinate respect for authority. In spite of his copious use of these 'facts,' however, Rabelais was not among the many eminent men of science of his time, and even after, who still remained unable to unshackle their spirit from the dead hand of the ancient past. Quite the contrary; with a species of ingratitude, so to say, he assails his sources on the score of credibility. Elianus he calls "tiercelet de menterie," and not even Pliny, from whom he borrowed so extensively, escaped the shafts of his satirical skepticism.

The function of the marvelous in the romances is to astound and enrapture the reader by transporting him from the world of harsh reality into a new world where the impossible is the rule, but an impossible made palatable by being transmuted and glorified through the fervent glow of the poetic imagination. The rôle the marvelous plays in the romances varies within the

---

[1] For his modern attitude toward the great questions he discusses, see Smith, *Rabelais in his Writings*, and A. F. Chappell, *The Enigma of Rabelais, an Essay in Interpretation* (1924). Chappell deals particularly with Rabelais' philosophical and religious views.

widest possible limits: in the *Lancelot du Lac*, for example, its part is a palmary one; whereas in *Méliadus de Leonnoys*, in *Gliglois*, and in *Durmart* it is altogether absent. Then in between these two extremes it frequently is found reduced to subordinate importance.

The Italians seized upon this particular feature of the romances, divorced it from the rest, and attached it to the heroes of the French epics, erecting it at the same time into a sacramental rule and giving it an extension only adumbrated in the Arthurian Romances. The peregrinations of the heroes become catalogues of stupendous adventures of all conceivable kinds, out of which invariably, either at the outset or eventually, they issue triumphant. Berni sums up, and not unfairly, in a four-line formula the substance and content of the Italian romances:

> Di giardino in giardino di ponte in ponte,
> Di lago in lago, e d'un in altro affano
> Ora è condotto il Principe, ora il Conte
> E come voi vedete allegri vanno.

> *—Orlando innamorato*, XXXIV, 1.

With the later Italians, with Pulci, Bojardo, Berni, and Ariosto, this exaggeration of the marvelous, carried out into the grotesque, was very probably not without its satirical intention. With respect to Folengo there can be no difference of opinion; his burlesque *Macaronics* are very obviously a grotesque satire, of both the French romances and those of his Italian predecessors.

While, however, the influence of the Italians on Rabelais is very manifest, it is less obvious in his treatment of the marvelous, the most essential characteristic of the Italian romances. Nor can we assign to the French romances a greater degree of influence on him in this respect. Nowhere does Rabelais' special ability in recreating a situation, in expanding the slightest hint, in adapting a *procédé*, in combining different and distinct models into something novel and peculiarly his own, appear to

better advantage. Rabelais' marvelous has no indubitable prototype, it has no counterpart, and in our day of universal sophis-
tication it can have no comparable imitation.

But before he evolved the process so well suited to his genius,
and compatible with its limitations, his imagination, which never
soars, oscillated more or less uncertainly between the marvelous
of the Italian romances and the marvelous of the chap-books of
the day, the latter exercising by far a preponderant influence.
In his later books (Books III, IV, v), he absolutely emancipated
himself from this uncongenial influence, and struck out in an
entirely new direction.   He turned his eyes from the *Morgante,*
from the *Orlando innamorato,* from the *Orlando furioso,* from
Folengo's Macaronic poems, and finally from the *Grandes Chroniques,* and directed them toward Elianus, toward Pliny, toward
the *Novus Orbis,* and the many recitals of fabulous medieval
journeys on the ocean, chief among them Saint Brendan's. These
sea journeys constitute the frame on which he wove his curious
lore of fishes, birds, beasts, and plants. At this juncture the
words of Lazare Sainéan may aptly be quoted:

> Là où les commentateurs n'ont vu jusqu'ici [V, 30–31] qu'une nomen-
> clature chaotique, il s'agit d'un excellent résumé des connaissances de
> l'époque, d'un document scientifique de premier ordre.   En ce qui touche
> l'histoire naturelle son oeuvre nous présente un tableau à peu près complet.
> Aucun fait saillant, d'ordre historique ou social, ne semble avoir échappé à
> son intelligence ouverte, à sa curiosité insatiable.   Grâce aux nombreux
> éléments épars dans son livre, nous avons été à même de reconstituer les
> principaux aspects de l'histoire naturelle depuis l'antiquité, en traversant le
> moyen âge et la Renaissance, jusqu'au milieu du seizième siècle.[2]

From the preceding paragraphs the reader may conclude
that while the marvelous runs through all of Rabelais' five
books, it does not show unity of conception and of execution
as in the romances before him, nor does it circumscribe itself
within the bounds of the grotesque and the impossible.   On the
contrary it is eclectic, its sources are many and not one, it is
inspired by the French and to a slight extent by the Italian
romances, by the popular romances, by the pseudo-science of

---

[2] *R. S. S.*, VI, 84.

antiquity and the Middle Ages, and by classical and medieval literature. For convenience of treatment it may be classified as:

    (*a*) The grotesque-marvelous,

    (*b*) The magical-marvelous,

    (*c*) The biological-marvelous,

    (*d*) The literary-marvelous,

    (*e*) And finally the marvelous of Rabelais' own invention.

As previously remarked, the grotesque element in Rabelais' marvelous has two sources: the Italian romances and the popular romances. It is not always possible to assign to each its proportionate share, as to a considerable extent they overlap. Consequently a differentiation of sources as between these two would add nothing to our understanding and appreciation of this aspect of the question.

In choosing giants for personages in his books, Rabelais had ample precedent. Giants, it is true, play an extremely restricted part in the Arthurian Romances, though they are not complete strangers to the French epic in rôles of more than minor importance. The giants of epic and romance, however, were far from having attained the prodigious stature they were made to assume later. We must come to Pulci· and the *Grandes Chroniques* before encountering for the first time the proximate prototypes of Rabelais' giants. Pulci says Morgante is "like a mountain," although he soon after finds no difficulty in walking through the doors of a monastery. With a pine tree as a spit, he roasts an elephant and devours it at one sitting; afterwards using the spit for a toothpick. With his bell-clapper he lays out about him five thousand Saracens. But multiplication of these details would be wearisome, since it is rather to the *Grandes Chroniques* that we must look for Rabelais' model. In them, when Merlin leaves Grandgousier and Galamelle, they shed enough tears to run two mills. The boy Gargantua throws stones at birds, each of which is as large as a millstone. The switch with which he urges his mare in his journey from the East to Arthur's court is as large as the mast of a ship. At Paris he sits on one of the towers of Notre Dame and his feet dip in the Seine. In combat against five hundred knights of the king of Ireland he catches them up and puts them away in various parts of his clothing; in a later fight he picks up a giant eighteen cubits high and tucks him away in his pouch. Rabelais' Gargantua, too, sits on the selfsame tower, and likewise Pantagruel sheds tears as large as ostrich eggs. In his expedition against the Dipsodes he walks with his head above the clouds, while he shelters his army against a sudden shower by covering it with his tongue. Maître Alco-fribas spends six months exploring Pantagruel's interior, in which he finds many thriving cities and states.

Quite in keeping with the physical dimensions of Rabelais' giants are their years and intellectual proportions. Gargantua, for example, has attained the age of "four hundred fourscore forty and four years" when Pantagruel is born. At the age of fifty-eight he begins his education in earnest with Ponocrates. Under this accomplished preceptor he does not leave unexplored or untried a single field of knowledge, or a single one of the manly exercises and games. His workday begins at four in the morning and continues far into the night. In these hours he executes a prodigious program, covering languages, literature, sacred and profane, arts and sciences, chivalric exercises, hunt-ing, swimming, and playing.

Illustrations of the same tenor might be indefinitely multi-plied, but would add little to the reader's understanding of this phase of the marvelous in Rabelais.[3]

Side by side with the grotesque-marvelous, Rabelais employs the magical-marvelous, though in a greatly attenuated form. This species of the marvelous demands a poetic feeling and imagination to which Rabelais was very largely a stranger. Accordingly, illustrations of the magical are not numerous in his books, and, with a sole exception, are distinctly trivial.

---

[3] In this connection the reader is referred to Pierre Villey's *Marot et Rabelais* (1923), 170–174, where Rabelais' use of a very frequent *procédé* is pointed out: that the incredible is made to assume the appearance of the credible by the copious use of precise details. In addition, the more roman-tic an author's material is the more concrete his vocabulary may need to be.

Frère Jean's exploits in chasing Picrochole's men from the vineyards of Seuillé earn for him an invitation to Grandgousier's castle, where Gargantua has just arrived from Paris. After an evening of wining, Gargantua and his companions, among them Frère Jean, set out at midnight on a reconnoissance. Very shortly after they chance upon a similar party from Picrochole's camp, under the command of Captain Tiravant. On discovering them, the doughty Frère Jean shouts: "Charge, devils, charge!" The enemy, on hearing this battle cry, verily thinking they have to do with devils, take to flight, with the exception of Captain Tiravant, who, "settling his lance in rest, hit the monk with all his might on the very middle of his breast, but coming against his horrific frock, the point of the iron flattened, as a wax candle would if struck against an anvil."

Weapons or armor possessing magical qualities rendering the wearer irresistible and invulnerable, while they are found in all primitive literature, reach their highest development in the Italian romances. It is true now and then they may be found in the French romances, for example the three shields the Lady of the Lake sends to Lancelot at the outset of his chivalric career, or Guenevere's shield, which possesses curative qualities.[4] But in general they play a minor rôle in Arthurian Romance, as the heroes of Arthur's court considered it a disgrace to possess an unfair advantage over an adversary. So we find Lancelot almost immediately discarding his shields. The Italians felt no such scruples, however, and in consequence, their heroes are often the possessors of enchanted swords, shields, lances, helmets, which are a source of envy and discord, and occasion extensive travels on the part of Saracen princes, who leave their seats in Asia and journey to Charlemagne's court to win them from their owners.

---

4 On the magical elements in the Old French romances, see Benjamin de la Waar Easter, *A Study of the Magic Elements in the Romans d'Aventure and the Romans Bretons* (Johns Hopkins dissertation, 1906). The first half only of this dissertation has been published.

In the single combat between Loupgarou and Pantagruel,
the latter almost comes to grief through Loupgarou's mace of
steel. It would seem that this tremendous weapon, weighing
"nine thousand seven hundred quintals and two quarterons,"
was formidable enough without being made more so by the
tricks of magic. But, in fact, "it was enchanted in such sort
that it could never break, but contrarily all that it did touch, did
break immediately." Knowing this, Pantagruel begins the combat
with a prayer to God and a vow to have his gospel preached in
Utopia and elsewhere if he proved successful. The vow was no
sooner made than there was heard a voice from heaven saying:
Hoc fac et vinces. In the course of the combat, Pantagruel's
weapon, a huge mast weighted with salt and wine, comes slightly
in contact with the stock of Loupgarou's mace, and breaks into
pieces. Great then is the distress of the good Pantagruel.
"Panurge, where art thou?" he shouts, and the faithful
Panurge would gladly have run to his master's aid had not
Loupgarou's giant escort hindered him. Pantagruel, however,
gives Loupgarou a kick in the belly which sends him heels over
head on the ground. The other giants run to Loupgarou's
assistance, whereupon Pantagruel seizes his prostrate adversary
by the feet and so belabors the rescuers that they are laid out
on the ground, where Panurge, Carpalim, and Eusthenes dis-
patch them by cutting their throats. Unfortunately, in the
fracas Epistemon is beheaded by a flying freestone forming
part of Loupgarou's armor. But Panurge's skill and cunning
are equal to the occasion. He carefully washes Epistemon's
truncated head in white wine, powders it, and joins it to the
body, adjusting carefully vein to vein, nerve to nerve. Next he
anoints the wound with a magical ointment, and fastens the
two parts of the body together with fifteen or sixteen stitches.
Epistemon soon comes back to life and gives an extraordinary
relation of what he has seen in the brief minutes spent in the
lower regions. There everything is topsy turvy, and the estate
and condition of the tenants is changed after a very strange

manner. The mighty are humbled: Xerxes is a huckster of mustard; Cyrus, a cowherd; Aeneas, a cabinetmaker. The humble are exalted: Diogenes struts about in a purple robe, with a scepter in his right hand; Jean le Maire counterfeits the pope, and kings and princes kiss his foot.

This episode of a lopped-off head being rejoined to its body is extremely common in medieval literature; it has its source in folklore.[5] It is found in the Irish sagas, in more than one Middle English poem, and in several Old French romances. The *Orlando innamorato* (Berni, LXII, 61) and the *Orlando furioso* (XV, 65 *seq.*) make use of it in a modified form. But in none of these must we look for Rabelais' prototype. It is probably to be found in a story, now lost, but also retold in Malory's *Morte D'Arthur* (VII, 22), in combination with a descent to Hell occurring in a dialogue of Lucian, the *Necyomantia*. In Malory, Gareth has a midnight appointment in Sir Gringamor's castle with Dame Lyones. Lynette, Lyones' sister, wishing to hinder the accomplishment of the lovers' desires, sends a knight, who attacks and wounds Gareth but in turn has his head stricken off. Lynette anoints the wound, and joins the head to the body, to which it sticks as fast as ever.[6] The stitches in the version of the *Pantagruel* are just such a surgical turn as we might expect from realistic Doctor Rabelais. In the *Necyomantia*, Mennipus relates to Philonides his visit to Hell, where, precisely as in Rabelais, the condition of the mighty of earth is lowly. Kings and satraps are humbled. He sees Philip of Macedon in a corner mending old slippers; and Xerxes and Darius begging alms at crossroads. Diogenes, on the other hand, is happy, and greets the laments of his neighbors and companions, over their low estate, with bursts of laughter.[7]

---

[5] For a study of the "Beheading *motif*" in medieval romance, see George L. Kittredge, *Gawain and the Green Knight* (Cambridge, 1916).

[6] Kittredge observes, p. 266, that this episode is not a version of the Beheading Game.

[7] For a review of the various descents to Hell, see Fleury, *Rabelais et ses oeuvres*, I, 398–411; and Edgar Blochet, *Sources orientales de la Divine Comédie* (Paris, 1901).

Plattard has observed, and perhaps justly, that Rabelais felt that the naïve efforts of the popular romances to awaken the wonder of the reader soon become monotonous, and defeat their very end.   Whether that be the cause, or the lapse of eleven years between the first part of Rabelais' work (Books I, II) and its last part (Books III, IV, V) had brought to maturity his fundamental qualities—his predilection for science, his realism, his skepticism—we have to record a complete change in his last three books in his treatment of the marvelous.   Magic is absolutely pretermitted in them, and even the physical proportions of his hero, though they are briefly indicated directly or indirectly four times, are without influence on the action. From now on Rabelais will draw from his wide scientific reading and immense erudition the material for his marvelous.   He will lay under contribution botany, and especially zoology, for the recondite lore by means of which he will make the reader marvel.   It is true the grotesque appears now and then in the later books, as in the stories of Bringuenarilles and Quaresmeprenant, but in these cases it is kept far in the background, since Rabelais does not directly introduce these worthies into his narrative.   It does get into the main current of the action in the episode of the Chitterlings, and with the Island of Ruach; but with the Chitterlings—and this is true also of Quaresmeprenant—the intention is so obviously allegorical that an attempt at classification must not be too rigidly pressed.

Pantagruel, with his company, sets out of the harbor of Thalasse in twelve ships on a Saint Brendan's journey to Utopia in quest of the Divine Bottle.   He has the precaution to load his fleet with large quantities of *Pantagruelion*.   Rabelais is at great pains to give a minute description of this herb, which Pantagruel discovered and of which he has taught mankind the uses.   The reader, unless a skilled botanist, would never recognize the herb *Pantagruelion* as flax.   Nowhere does Rabelais call it that; on the contrary, he stresses the fire-resisting qualities of one of its species, and calls it variously *Asbeston, Pantagruelion Carpasien Asbestin,* and *Pantagruelion Asbeste.*   The purpose of his long and detailed description is perfectly obvious. Equally so is the phrase "as divine as it is mysterious," which he applies to its uneven phyllotaxy, represented by him by the odd numbers 5 and 7. As a last fanciful touch he adds: "On sème cestuy Pantagruelion à la nouvelle venue des hirondelles, on le tire de terre lorsque les cigalles commencent à s'enrouer,"—a fanciful way of saying it is sowed in the early spring and gathered in the early fall.[8]

This *procédé* of mock concealment of the identity of a common and homely animal or plant under long descriptions of its appearance, its qualities, and its uses, to deceive the science of the reader and to awaken his interest and wonder, is not novel nor singular, and skilfully done as it is by Rabelais, it may be very effective. Rabelais employs it but once, as the other plants he introduces to us are sufficiently marvelous in themselves not to need the rhetorical tricks of the writer. Such is the herb Gaster shows Pantagruel whereby he conjures rain from the skies, merely by cutting it in the meadows where it grows; or the herb *Erigeron,* which, put in the mouth of the hindmost of a flock of fleeing sheep, will quickly bring all of them to a stop; or the herb *Ethiopis,* which will open any lock near which it is placed; or the herb which will draw an ax out of a tree, howsoever deep it may be struck into it—woodpeckers use it to open their holes in tree trunks after they have been closed by an iron wedge. No less magical are the properties of the *Dittany,* by eating which bucks eject from their bodies the arrows with which they have been pierced; or of the laurel and the fig tree, whose odors have the power to turn aside the thunderbolt.

On the fourth day after setting out from Thalasse the company reach the beautiful Island of Medamothi. It is a great mart for the Afro-Asiatic trade. There Pantagruel and his companions purchase many curiosities, chief among them

---

[8] See Méon, *Roman du Renart (Renart le Nouvel)* IV, 276: "Ces letres furent kierkies l'an ke li moussons se combatirent as mouskerons, sietante et set el mois que li pouchin devienent poulet." Also IV, 306: "Ces letres furent faites et kierkies l'an que wesples et li tahon se combatirent sour le Mont de Liban, nonante et un, el mois que les ruines foursent."

an animal called the "Tarand." Rabelais' description of this animal, which has been identified with the reindeer, is taken mainly from Pliny, but to Pliny he has added many fanciful details of his own. The reputed cameleon qualities of the "Tarand" are explained by the fact that it shows variations in color, many becoming white in winter. The reindeer was practically unknown in France in the sixteenth century, and consequently Rabelais could safely expand Pliny's already bizarre description without shocking the common credulity.

Several days after leaving Medamothi the fleet anchors at the "Isle Ennasin." Here we are consciously introduced by Rabelais into a new world, and never after does he allow us to forget this. The Ennasins address the company as "vous aultres gens de l'aultre monde," and in the following chapters to the end of Book v variations of this phrase are continually before our eyes: "vous aultres gens transpontins" (IV, 49), "les universités de vostre monde" (IV, 53), "en vostre monde" (V, 5), "vous aultres de l'autre monde" (V, 7), etc. We are now well on the broad and open bosom of the medieval ocean, where strange peoples and strange sights await us in each chapter. For our purpose we need land with Pantagruel and his company only on the Island of Ruach, and afterwards not until we reach the Country of Satin (v, 30–31).

After their departure from the Isle of the Ennasins the company experience several adventures, noteworthy among them the episode between Panurge and Dindenault and his sheep, and the great storm that would have irretrievably wrecked the expedition but for Pantagruel's and Frère Jean's courage and stoutness. Soon after they reach the Isle of Ruach. They discover the inhabitants to be a queer sort: they drink nothing, they eat nothing save wind. With them windmills are at a premium and the wealthy are wont to banquet around tables spread under one or two of them. At such times they eulogize the sirocco, the zephyr, the sou'wester, the norther, for their excellence, salubrity, and rarity, each as his own taste in winds prompts him. Unfortunately, Bringuenarilles, a near neighbor, frequently resorts to their island for his health, on which occasions he devours innumerable mills. Pantagruel is happy to be able to tell them Bringuenarilles has just died from swallowing a spat of butter before a warm oven on the advice of his physician.[9]

Several days after leaving Ruach, while the questers were feasting and at the same time learnedly discoursing, Pantagruel jumped to his feet and assumed a listening attitude. Soon the others of the company began distinguishing the noises and sounds that had first attracted their leader's attention; no one was in sight, but gradually the air became filled with the shouts of men, with the wails of women and children, with the neighing of horses, and finally with all the multitudinous sounds of a battle. The pilot explained that they were now on the confines of the Glacial Sea, where the winter before a great battle had occurred between the Arimaspiens and the Nephelibates. These outcries, and lamentations, and the tumult of battle were frozen then, and now were melting under the summer sun and becoming once more audible. Pantagruel scooped up with his hands sounds of various sorts, threw them on the deck. In appearance they were like sugar plums and various in color; on melting they liberated words in a barbaric tongue.

After weeks of traveling, in which Pantagruel's prognostication that "no melancholy would be encountered on the way" (III, 47) is fully borne out, the company at last arrive in the Country of Satin.

This land, appropriately enough, is placed at the other end of the world, and thus may quite suitably be selected as the home of the exotic and the unreal. With Rabelais the phrase Country of Satin—possibly from the figuration on tapestries of mythological subjects — seems to have denoted a non-existent country. In IV, 7, Panurge, while pushing Dindenault's servants back into the sea in which they found themselves through

---

[9] Cf. the burlesque deaths of other giants: Margutte dies of bursting from laughter, Morgante from the bite of a small crab, *Morgante maggiore,* XIX, 149; XX, 51–52.

his cunning, mockingly wished them that they might, like Jonah, be swallowed by a whale and on the third day disgorged safe and sound in some country of satin. In this imaginary land by far the greatest number of Rabelais' animals, birds, fishes, and reptiles find a home. They are represented in order on tapestries of velvet and damask. They fall into two classes:

(a) Real animals, birds, and reptiles, among them the elephant and the rhinoceros, exotics in France at the time, and known only to a few travelers;

(b) Imaginary animals, birds, and reptiles, such as the unicorn, the phoenix and many others.

Animals so well known as the elephant is today could in 1550 quite suitably be relegated to a country of satin, for at that time the elephant had, so far as is known, never been seen in France by a Frenchman. Its first description *d'après nature* by a Frenchman was that of Pierre Gilles[10] toward the middle of the sixteenth century, who had seen it in Constantinople. Of course, the elephant was known by hearsay in France long before then, and as a matter of fact under the various names 'elefant,' 'oliphant' and 'oriflant' is found embalmed in many an Old French poem side by side with other unknown but real animals.

Naturally this universal ignorance in Europe of exotic animals afforded writers plenty of elbow room for the exercise of their imagination. Here is the fantastic description of the elephant Philippe de Thaün gives us in his Bestiary (1541–1550):

> Es jambes par nature
> N'en a qu'une juinture,
> Il ne pot pas gesir
> Quand il se volt dormir;
> Kar se culchiez esteit
> Par sei ne levereit,
> E en liu de culchier
> Li estot apuier
> U a arbre u a mur
> Idonc dort a seur.

---

[10] Celebrated physician and naturalist, and a contemporary of Rabelais.

Many writers, among them Pliny, showed much the same credulity as to the appearance and habits of the elephant, and of them Rabelais scornfully remarks that they had never seen it except in painting.[11]

Four centuries after Philippe, these animals could still be described quite imaginatively. Berni, among others, endows exotics with huge dimensions and extraordinary attributes; as, for instance, the giraffe:

> Una giraffa....
> Scrivel Turpino, e poca gente il crede,
> Ch'undici braccia era del muso al piede.
>
> —*Orl. inn.*, LVII, 38.

His elephant is of no more modest proportions:

> Uscito fuora un re de gli elefanti
> L'autor lo dice, ed io creder nol posso,
> Che trenta palmi er alto e venti grosso.
>
> —*Ibid.*, LVII, 41.

Almost a hundred years later, Montaigne could express astonishment at the sight of a tiger which he saw in Florence, although as early as 1534 several of them had been presented to Francis I by the Turkish Emir Khair Eddin, then on an embassy at his court: "Nous vismes là," he writes, "....un animal de la grandeur d'un fort grand mastin, de la forme d'un chat, tout martelé de blanc et de noir, qu'ils nomment tigre." Apparently, in Rabelais' opinion, the elephant in its actuality was a marvelous enough animal not to need to be magnified by the imagination. At all events, he gives of it an accurate description.

To the Country of Satin Rabelais relegates, among others, the cameleon, the pelican, the panther, the reindeer, the aurochs, the hyena, the giraffe, the gazelle, and the tiger, all of them virtually unknown in France in his day.

---

[11] Curiously enough, the entire passage from Philippe seems to be a literal translation of Caesar's description of the marvelous elk that inhabited, it was popularly believed, the Hercynian forest (*De Bello Gallico*, VI, 27).

Nor does he fail to avail himself of occult and supernatural powers attributed to real animals in his time and long after. Owing to the superstition with which they were regarded, he fittingly places in the Country of Satin the remora, which was credited with the ability to stop a ship in its course and to draw up gold fallen into wells; the halcyon, which even Montaigne believed had the power to still the sea; the seal,[12] which was thought to be able to turn aside the thunderbolt, and whose skin, it was believed in the Middle Ages, rendered the wearer invulnerable; the gnu, with the venomous eyes that could kill.

Tilley points out[13] that Rabelais drew from the *Novus Orbis* his description of the elephant, and assigns the same source for his description of the unicorn. In this fabulous animal, which with the rhinoceros and the hippopotamus he had already placed in the Abbey of Thélème ''en peinture,'' Tilley sees a fusion on Rabelais' part of two animals described in the *Novus Orbis*, the first the rhinoceros, described evidently from personal observation by Marco Polo; the second, a mysterious one-horned animal which Varthema saw in the Temple of Mecca. A comparison of Rabelais' description with the passages from the *Novus Orbis* shows conclusive concordances. Tilley's remarks may be supplemented, however, with a text from *Renart le Novel*,[14] showing that these two animals long before had become confused in the popular mind, owing, doubtless, to their possessing each a single horn in the middle of the forehead.

Other imaginary animals placed in the Country of Satin are the wer-wolf; the centaur; the manticorne, found in the Bestiaries; the cucrocutes, also called leucrocutes, a cross between the hyena and the lioness; neades, at the sound of whose voice the earth opens into chasms; the basilisk, whose eye deals death;

---

[12] Gargantua's gloves are of sealskin, likewise the defensive armor of King Anarch's foot soldiers.

[13] *Mod. Lang. Rev.* (1906–1907), part ii, pp. 316–326.

[14] ll. 2110–2113:   Sire, pierdu aves Tibiert
Et ses deus fius, Rinoceron
L'Unicorne par Sant Symon,
Le singe Cointeriel ausi.

the hydra; the griffon; and the phoenix, belief in whose resuscitation from its own ashes persisted till the end of the sixteenth century.

At times Rabelais amuses himself by adding to the marvelous attributes of his animals and plants. In the case of the "Tarand," for instance, with respect to its ability to change color, with which it was generally credited, Rabelais adds these details:

.... Je l'ay vu couleur changer, non à l'approche seulement des choses colorées, mais de soy-mesmes, selon la peur ou affection qu'il avait. Comme sus un tapis vert je l'ay vu certainement verdoyer, mais y restant quelque espace de temps devenir jaune, bleu, tanne, violet par succès; en la facon que voyez la creste des coqs d'Inde couleur selon leurs passions changer (IV, 2).

Again he frequently expresses skepticism. "J'y vis un caméléon," he says, "tel que le descrit Aristoteles . . . . et ne vivait que d'air non plus que l'autre" (V, 30); and concerning the aphrodisiac qualities of the herb called *Targon:* "Ne m'allegues point l'Indian tant celebré par Theophraste, Pline et Atheneus, lequel avec l'aide de certaine herbe le faisait en un jour soixante et dix fois, et plus. Je n'en crois rien" (III, 27).

Several animals placed in the Country of Satin are apparently of Rabelais' own fabrication, such as La My-quaresmes, la My-aout, la My-mars, the "poissons d'avril," the "hallebardes gauchères," and "la beste à deux dos," which Shakespeare remembers in *Othello* (I, i). Finally the Country of Satin is made the sanctuary of two marvels of antiquity, the Golden Fleece and the hide of Apuleius' Golden Ass.

While not strictly pertinent, it may be asked what suggested to Rabelais the idea of the Country of Satin. Scarcely the Bestiaries, as the only analogy between them and Rabelais is that both deal with animals real and imaginary, but in an altogether different manner and spirit.[15] If Rabelais was directly

---

· [15] Cf. *Couronnement Renart*, III, 1708–1825, for a remarkable list of four-footed animals, real and imaginary, arranged alphabetically from a to z.

inspired, it probably was by Pulci. In the pavilion of gold and silk presented to Rinaldo by Luciana, Marsilio's daughter (*M.M.*, XIV, 42–86), on each of the four parts into which it is divided, a different aspect of natural history is represented:[16] on the first part, gems embroidered around seraphs, and cherubs; on the second part, fishes are represented in the sea, swimming about Neptune, Thetis, and Ulysses; and Triton too is there appeasing the tempest, and Glaucus, and Galatea, and the Trojan ships metamorphosed into nymphs; the fourth part represents the land with its great cities, its animals, and plants, and serpents. By far the greater part of animate creation figured on this tapestry is real. Throughout the forty-four stanzas very few forms of imaginary life appear, and even most of these were believed in at the time Pulci wrote, as, for instance, the phoenix. Now, if we turn to canto XXV, 311–332, of the same poem, we find another list of animals and reptiles enumerated by the demon Astaroth to Rinaldo and Ricciardetto on their journey through the air. This second list is made up, chiefly, of legendary animals and reptiles, along with several real animals not known at the time in Western Europe, such as the crocodile and the rhinoceros.

Comparing these two lists with Rabelais' Country of Satin, we will be struck with the following similarities:

(1) In the first list, Pulci represents his animals, reptiles, birds and fishes on tapestry, as does Rabelais.

(2) Pulci's two lists together enumerate practically all the animals, reptiles, etc., that we find in Rabelais, and many others besides.

(3) In both authors the various orders of the animal kingdom are segregated.

(4) The use of mythological personages in both Rabelais and Pulci.

------

16 For a description of tents figuring the natural kingdoms in embroidery, see *Roman de Thèbes*, 2925–2962; 3979–4068. Kings' pavilions were a favorite subject for rhetoric in the romances, so much so that the poet of *Ider* is moved to protest against this pedantic fashion (see G. Paris, *Histoire littéraire de la France*, XXX, 210).

(5) In at least two cases Rabelais translates almost word for word Pulci's description of imaginary animals: the animal he calls "cucrocute" he takes from Pulci, XXV, 313, where it is called "leucrocuta," and the serpent he calls "catoblepe" Rabelais takes from XXV, 314, where it is called by the same name. Other similarities that could be noted may be accidental.

(6) Both Rabelais and Pulci dismiss the fishes summarily.

Undoubtedly Pulci, in constituting his lists, drew extensively on the Bestiaries, as is evident from qualities he attributes to the phoenix, the pelican, the beaver, and the unicorn. Rabelais, in re-working Pulci's enumerations, brought to the task a much more extensive fund of general and specific knowledge gathered from Pliny and Aristotle among the ancients; from Avicenna and Albertus Magnus among the writers of the Middle Ages; and from various sources of his own time, several of whom he mentions in his Country of Satin in the following terms:

En un coing là près vismes Aristoteles tenant une lanterne .... Derrière lui estoient comme records de sergents plusieurs autres philosophes .... Entre iceux j'y advisay Pierre Gilles, lequel tenait un urinal en main considérant en profonde contemplation l'urine de ces beaux poissons (v, 31).

In the preceding chapter he says:

J'y vis un caméléon, tel que le descrit Aristoteles, et tel que me l'avoit quelquefois monstré Charles Marais, medecin insigne en la noble cité de Lyon. . . .;

and of the rhinoceros:

J'y vis un rhinoceros du tout semblable à celui que Henry Clerberg[17] m'avait autrefois monstré ....

From the last two quotations we may fairly assume, predisposed thereto as we are by what otherwise we know of Rabelais' universal scholarship, insatiable curiosity, and extensive information in unusual and recondite fields, that he lost no opportunity to supplement and control his bookish knowledge of natural history by personal observation. Such opportunities did not fail to present themselves during his many voyages to Italy. In

---

[17] A German settled in Lyons, and one of its most famous merchants. Knighted by Francis I.

one passage at least (IV, 11), he broadly hints at a visit paid the celebrated zoological gardens of the Strozzi in Florence, where many animals, exotics then in France, could be seen. Charles VIII, too, in 1494, visited the famous menagerie, and was struck by nothing in that city so much as by the lions he saw there.

The writers of the Italian comic romances, owing to the fact that their fictions are exaggerated beyond all precedent, and that they address themselves to audiences that have not remained entirely unsophisticated with the lapse of time, frequently interrupt themselves in the midst of the narration of their marvelous adventures long enough to invoke the final authority of Turpin. Again and again occur the formulae "scrivel Turpin," "Turpin lo dice," "l'autor lo dice," until themselves they become infected with the burlesque spirit. Such formulae, of course, were universally used in the Middle Ages, but without burlesque content, and purely as a literary convention, except perhaps in the very earliest times. Rabelais too feels the need of some sanction for his marvelous, and he makes more than once an effort to present it. If he tells us the infant Pantagruel had a cow for a wet nurse it is because, so he says, he finds this statement in the 'history' he used as a source (II, 4); if Gargantua's mare is as large as "six oriflans" and has cloven hoofs, it is because she is a product of Africa, "and Africa, as every one knows, is always productive of some new wonder" (I, 16; V, 3); his giants find their sanction in literary usage and popular belief. So also with the Country of Satin. His authority for such a land, peopled with the curiosities with which he fills it, is the hunchbacked, misshapen, and monstrous old man Hearsay, whose mouth is split back to his ears, who has seven tongues and each cleft into seven parts. About his head, and on various other parts of his body, he has as many ears distributed as Argus had eyes; as for the rest, he is blind and paralyzed in his limbs. Hearsay is the presiding divinity of

this strange land, and around him Maître Alcofribas saw men
and women in multitudes, all of them listening reverently to the
babel issuing from his forty-nine tongues in divers languages.
Among them he recognized Herodotus, Pliny, Strabo, Jacques
Cartier, Marco Polo, Pietro Alvarez, to mention only a few. The
allegory is obvious; and equally so is Rabelais' satirical intent.
The Country of Satin is a satire on travelers' tales;[18] on those
who write incredible relations on hearsay. In fine, the Country
of Satin constitutes a most striking illustration of Rabelais'
universal skepticism.[19]

---

[18] J. C. Dunlop, *History of Fiction* (ed. 2, Edinburgh, 1816), III, 74,
assigns as one of the "four things Rabelais principally seems to have
proposed to ridicule .... the lying and extravagant tales then in vogue."

[19] Lazare Sainéan's articles on natural history in Rabelais, appearing
in the *R. S. S.*, have been extensively drawn upon in the preparation of
this chapter.

CHAPTER VII

CONCLUSIONS

The obvious difference in manner and style between the two parts of Rabelais' work is, it is now clear, a natural consequence of their method of composition, which was, so far as concerns the first two books, entirely casual. In the *Gargantua* and the *Pantagruel* we find a repetition of manner, and, in a large measure, a repetition of content: both show the same characteristics of form, in both the history of the heroes is developed within the framework of the Arthurian Romance; again, the subject matter of the one to a considerable extent overlaps that of the other. With this repetition, naturally enough, is found, besides increased mastery of technique, a great advance in the clarity and precision of Rabelais' ideas. This is true particularly of the parts of the two books which ventilate his views on education, war, and monkery. In the *Pantagruel* his ideas on these important questions are not yet sharply defined: he felt, accordingly, the necessity of restating them in the *Gargantua*. The new scheme of education, for example, only adumbrated in the *Pantagruel,* is set forth at length in the first book and in much sharper contrast with the old education which the Sorbonne championed. In the second place, Rabelais offers in Thélème an ideal substitute for the narrow discipline, intellectual as well as physical, of the monasteries in which the old ideal was entrenched. What has just been said of education and monachism is equally true of war, three questions which constitute almost the entire matter of the first two books.

When once more, a decade later, Rabelais felt the urge to give currency to a new and more varied set of ideas, he recognized that the form which he had already twice used had grown inadequate, and he found himself under the necessity of selecting a new vehicle for their expression. He found it ready at hand in the form of such Grail romances as *L'hystoire* and the two *Questes,* a form which with simplicity united great flexibility. It is indeed well suited to present a succession of tableaux with no logical connection between them, which can be multiplied and expanded at will. At the same time, the Grail itself, symbolical of spiritual perfection in the romances, could readily be made the symbol of the thirst for universal knowledge and for truth that characterized so many humanists of the Renaissance, and especially Rabelais himself.

Rabelais solved, as happily as possible under the circumstances, the problem of articulating the first part of his work with the second by the expedient of using and, after his usual manner, expanding one of the commonest incidents found in the Arthurian Romances of the biographical type as well as of the Grail-quest type. The dream of Panurge and the consultation held to explain it link up fairly well with Book II through one of the incidents that Rabelais had promised to treat in his "continuation," the marriage of Panurge and his cuckolding, and on the other with the quest of the oracle and the Holy Bottle, which the third book inaugurates. He found, besides, minor means of cementing the first and the second parts together, such as, for instance, using the same personages throughout his work.

The critics who have seen in Rabelais' work mainly an imitation of the Gest Romances were probably misled by two facts: (a) he makes a greater parade of this type of romance in the first two books than of the Arthurian Romances, and (b) war apparently plays a primary rôle in the *Gargantua* and the *Pantagruel.* If we turn to the second chapter, it will be seen that as against three Arthurian Romances that Rabelais seems without doubt to have known at first hand, he gives positive indications of having read as many as eight Gest Romances. Furthermore, the number and the definiteness of the allusions that he makes to the Gest Romances quite obscure his references to the Arthurian Romances, which seldom are specific or arresting. As for the two wars in Rabelais, their importance, it has been pointed out, may easily be exaggerated. Considered from their proper angle—

from the angle of their literary function—they immediately assume their true value and perspective: they appear as one of the many and various phases of the exploits of the hero, a phase which is a frequent, or even usual, but seldom an organic, part of the Arthurian Romances.

The Gest Romance, on the other hand, stresses almost exclusively the warlike exploits of the hero. From the outset war is made the chief 'matter' of this type of romance, and it invariably shows impatience to get down to what is properly its primary concern. The usual formal divisions of the Arthurian Romance — Ancestry, Youth and Education, Exploits, Marriage — are foreign to the Gest Romance. It is true that in a few of these, like *Ogier le Danois* and *Godefroy de Bouillon,* a feeble attempt is made to furnish the hero with an Ancestry and a Youth — not however with an Education — but in the one this part of the romance is so brief and perfunctory and in the other so chaotic that it can safely be said that they could not have furnished Rabelais with a model for these very clear-cut divisions of his romance. In the second place, the elaborate Arthurian Romance background that Rabelais is at such pains to build up in his first two books is almost wholly wanting in the Gest Romance. On the other hand, both in the Arthurian Romances and in Rabelais, we find, in addition to the formal resemblances just pointed out, a large place given to the background: the daily life of their personages, and the political, religious, and social usages of the times, whereas these are scanted in the Gest Romances. Finally, the sense of exotism and mystery which is characteristic of the Grail-quest romances especially, while all but unknown to the Gest Romance, is consciously and faithfully reproduced in Rabelais.

Characteristic of the Arthurian Romance too is the treatment of the marvelous. When the realistic Gest Romance ventures into that path, the effect usually is as of new bricks in an old wall, as for example the imprisonment of Ogier by Morgan la Fée; or there results complete dissonance, as in *Huon de Bordeaux,* where the first part is epic in character, chronicling the story of a feudal tragedy, whereas the second part, dealing with Huon's journey to Babylon in order to insult the admiral and cut off his beard, a feat which he accomplishes with the help of Oberon and his magic horn, plunges the reader into the world of purest romance.[1] Only rarely is the grafting of this romance characteristic on a story primarily epical in character successful enough to appear natural. Illustrations of successful grafting may be found in the Swan-Knight story of the *Helyas,* or ancestry phase of the *Godefroy de Bouillon,* and in the *Maugis d'Aigremont.*

Rabelais did not neglect to impart to his work this characteristic aspect of the romance. While the marvelous of the two parts of his work shows a fundamental cleavage, that of Books I and II being almost wholly the marvelous of the popular romances, whereas that of Books IV and V is primarily the marvelous of biological science in its primitive stage, nevertheless throughout his work his marvelous, derived though it be from such varied sources as legend, popular superstition, ancient and medieval writers, and from the accounts of travelers and explorers of his own day, is skilfully enough interwoven into the main threads of his story not to offend our sense of literary propriety. Only in the first two books, however, is the marvelous made to play a major and decisive rôle, the rôle it usually plays in the Arthurian Romances; if Rabelais clings to it in the second part of his work it is because it constitutes, in one form or another, a traditional and almost essential part of the romance. In the last two books he weaves it unobtrusively into his narrative and in such a way as to arouse the interest and pleasure even of the modern and sophisticated reader.

The satirical spirit of the Middle Ages, abounding in the grotesque and delighting in burlesque, parody, and caricature

---

[1] *Huon de Bordeaux* is an inexpert welding together of two distinct literary genres. This welding occurred before the story reached the Gest Romance stage. As Ker points out (*Epic and Romance, passim*), Romance in many varieties is to be found inherent in Epic. Mingling of romance with epic strains is not infrequent. But this mingling in the French epic gave rise to a relation of antagonism in which the older form gave way to the newer.

in all their forms, culminated in Rabelais. In him satire attains epic proportions. He pours into the mould of the Arthurian Romance a vast satirical 'review' of the persons, institutions, beliefs, in brief of the life of his own times.[2] A century and a half later we shall see Fénelon likewise pour into the mould of the Homeric epic—in the *Télémaque*—a critique of the persons and practices of his day, and try to lead his royal charge in the path leading to Utopia.

In his Utopia, Rabelais enshrined Truth and universal Knowledge. They, it has already been said, are the ultimate object of his quest. The Bottle, as its concrete and visible representation, is the symbol of the intellectual and spiritual renovation of man at the time of the Renaissance. The Rabelaisian quest is instinct with the breath and spirit that animated the Revival of Learning. Its first condition of success was complete freedom from the blind beliefs and superstitions which an uncritical age had bequeathed to a more enlightened one, and an open and inquiring mind unswayed by prejudices and prepossessions. Everything that was error or unreason found in him an adversary. Thus he ran counter to many beliefs in many men, in the "demoniacles Calvins" as well as the "enraigés Putherbes."

Fanatics of their stripe pursued him with all the hatred and venom that bigotry knows so well how to employ. Twice at least he was compelled to flee to foreign lands in order to escape burning at the stake. Yet it was after his two flights, after the warning implied in the terrible fate that overtook his friend Dolet, that he leveled his most telling blows against Error. In his day too often he was accused of buffoonery by men who should have known better. His buffoonery is just another bell-clapper like the one with which Morgante laid out the Saracens by the thousands about him; it is a huge, shattering lance that Rabelais the Crusader so well knew how to place in rest against his enemies in the great CRUSADE OF TRUTH.

---

[2] Excellent treatments of this aspect of Rabelais' work may be found in Lenient, *La Satire en France; ou la littérature militante du XVIe siècle*, I, chap. 2; and Schneegans, *Geschichte der grotesken Satire*.

BIBLIOGRAPHY

D'AVEZAC, M., "Les îles fantastiques de l'océan occidentale. Les îles de
   Saint Brendan," *Nouvelles annales des voyages et des sciences géo-
   graphiques*, I, Notice des découvertes faites au moyen âge dans
   l'Océan Atlantique (Paris, 1845).

BATIFFOL, LOUIS, *Le Siècle de la Renaissance* (ed. 2, Paris, 1911).

BIRCH-HIRSCHFELD, A., *Die Sage vom Graal* (Leipzig, 1877).

BLOCHET, EDGAR, *Les Sources orientales de la Divine Comédie* (Paris, 1901).

BROWN, A. C. L., "From Cauldron of Plenty to Grail," *Mod. Phil.*, XIV.
   "The Grail and the English Sir Perceval," *Mod. Phil.*, XVI, XVII,
   XVIII, XXII.

BRUCE, JAMES DOUGLAS, *The Evolution of Arthurian Romance*, 2 vols.
   (Baltimore, 1923).

CASTETS, FERD., *Recherches sur les rapports des chansons de geste et de
   l'épopée chevaleresque italienne* (Paris, 1887).

CHAMPFLEURY, *Histoire de la caricature au moyen âge et sous la Renaissance*, 1867–1871.

CHAPPELL, A. F., *The Enigma of Rabelais* (Cambridge University Press,
   1924).

COMPAYRE, G., *Histoire critique des doctrines de l'éducation en France*
   (Paris, 1879).

CONS, LOUIS, "Le Problème du cinquième livre du Pantagruel," *Revue
   bleue*, April 25, 1914.

DESJARDINS, A., *Les Moralistes français du seizième siècle* (Paris, 1870).

FLEURY, JEAN, *Rabelais et ses oeuvres* (Paris, 1877).

GAFFAREL, PAUL, "Les Voyages de Saint Brendan et des Papae dans
   l'Atlantique du moyen âge," *Bulletin de la Société de Géographie
   de Rochefort*, II (1880).

GAUTIER, LEON, *Les Epopées françaises* (ed. 2, Paris, 1878–1897).

GEBHART, EMILE, *Rabelais, la renaissance, et la réforme* (Paris, 1895).

DE GOEJE, M. J., *La légende de Saint Brendan* (Leiden, 1890).

GUILHERMOZ, P., *Essai sur l'origine de la noblesse en France* (Paris, 1902).

HERTZ, WILHELM, *Parzival von Wolfram von Eschenbach, neu bearbeitet*
   (Stuttgart, 1898).

JACOB, P. L., Le Bibliophile Jacob or Paul Lacroix, *Recherches biblio-graphiques* (Paris, 1880).

LACROIX, PAUL, *Science and Literature in the Middle Ages* (New York, 1878).

LEFRANC, ABEL, "Pantagruel explorateur," *Revue de Paris*, Feb. 1, 15, 1904.
Les Navigations de Pantagruel (Paris, 1905).
Numerous articles in the *R. E. R.* and *R. S. S.*

LENIENT, CHARLES, *La Satire en France au moyen âge* (ed. 4, Paris, 1893).
La Satire en France; ou la littérature militante au seizième siècle (ed. 3, Paris, 1886).

MARGRY, PIERRE, *Les Navigations françaises et la révolution maritime du XIVe au XVIe siècle* (Paris, 1867).

MEYER and NUTT, *The Voyage of Bran, son of Febal* (London, 1895–1897).

NEWELL, W. W., *The Legend of the Holy Grail* (Cambridge, Mass., 1902).

NITZE, WM. A., *Perlesvaus* (Johns Hopkins dissertation, 1902).
"The Fisher King in the Grail Romances," *P M L A* XXIV.
"*Sans et matiere* dans les oeuvres de Chrétien de Troyes," *Romania*, XLIV.

NUTT, ALFRED, *Studies on the Legend of the Holy Grail* (London, 1888).

PARIS, GASTON, in *Histoire littéraire de la France*, XXX, 14 *seq.*
La littérature française au moyen âge (1913).

PARIS, PAULIN, in *Histoire littéraire de la France*, XXII, 259 *seq.*
Les Romans de la Table Ronde, 5 vols. (Paris, 1868).

PLATTARD, JEAN, *L'oeuvre de Rabelais* (Paris, 1910).

POTVIN, CHARLES, *Perceval le Gallois, ou Le Conte du Saint Graal*, 6 vols. (Mons, 1866).

PUTNAM, GEORGE H., *Books and their Makers During the Middle Ages* (New York, 1898).

Revue des études rabelaisiennes, I–X.

Revue du seizième siècle, I–VI.

REGNIER, G., *Les Origines du roman réaliste* (Paris, 1912).

SCHNEEGANS, H., *Geschichte der grotesken Satire* (Strassburg, 1894).

SCHULTZ, ALWIN, *Das höfische Leben zur Zeit der Minnesinger* (Leipzig, 1889).

SEBILLOT, PAUL, *Gargantua dans les traditions populaires* (Paris, 1883).

SAINEAN, LAZARE, Numerous articles in *R.E.R.* and *R.S.S.*

SMITH, W. F., *Rabelais in his Writings* (Cambridge University Press, 1918). *The Works of Rabclais* translated into English (1893).

SOMMER, H. OSKAR, *The Vulgate Version of the Arthurian Romances,* 7 vols. (Washington, 1908–1914).

STAPFER, PAUL, *Rabelais, sa personne, son génie, son oeuvre* (Paris, 1889).

THOMPSON, J. W., *The Frankfort Book Fair* (Chicago, 1911).

THUASNE, LOUIS, *Etudes sur Rabelais* (Paris, 1904).

TILLEY, ARTHUR, "Rabelais and Geographical Discovery," *Mod. Lang. Rev.,* II, III, IV.
François Rabelais (Philadelphia and London, 1907).
R. S. S., VI, 61 *seq.*

VILLEY, PIERRE, *Marot et Rabelais* (Paris, 1923).

WAHLUND, CARL, *Die altfranzösische Prosaübersetzung von Brendans Meerfahrt* (Upsala, 1900).

WESTON, JESSIE, L., *The Legend of Sir Perceval,* 2 vols. (London, 1906–1909).
The Quest of the Holy Grail (London, 1913).
From Ritual to Romance (Cambridge, 1920).

WRIGHT, THOMAS, *Womankind in Western Europe from the Earliest Times to the Seventeenth Century* (London, 1869).
A History of Caricature and the Grotesque in Literature and Art (London, 1875).

INDEX